E. J. W. GIBB MEMORIAL

SERIES

NEW SERIES, XXIX

Document Forms for Official Orders of Appointment in the Mughal Empire

Translation, Notes and Text

John F. Richards
Professor of History, Duke University

PUBLISHED AND DISTRIBUTED BY THE
TRUSTEES OF THE "E. J. W. GIBB MEMORIAL"

1st Edition 1986

ISBN 0 906094 14 3

Printed and bound by The Burlington Press (Cambridge) Ltd, Foxton, Cambridge

Produced in association with Book Production Consultants, Cambridge, England

This Volume is one
of a Series
Published by the Trustees of the

"E. J. W. GIBB MEMORIAL"

The Funds of this Memorial are derived from the Interest accruing from a Sum of money given by the late MRS. GIBB of Glasgow, to perpetuate the Memory of her beloved Son

ELIAS JOHN WILKINSON GIBB

and to promote those researches into the History, Literature, Philosophy and Religion of the Turks, Persians and Arabs, to which, from his Youth upwards, until his premature and deeply lamented Death in his forty-fifth year, on December 5, 1901, his life was devoted.

تِلْكَ آثَارُنَا تَدُلُّ عَلَيْنَا * فَانْظُرُوا بَعْدَنَا إِلَى الآثَارِ

"These are our works, these works our souls display;
Behold our works when we have passed away."

CLERK OF THE TRUST
P. R. Bligh, F.C.A.
c/o Spicer and Pegler
Leda House, Station Road
Cambridge, England

Table of Contents

Note on Transliteration

The system employed is either that of Steingass in his *Persian-English Dictionary* or, infrequently, that of Platts, in *A Dictionary of Urdu, Classical Hindi and English.*

Preface and Acknowledgements

This work provides access to a compilation of Mughal administrative document forms in both translation and text. I offer it in the hope that it will be useful to those historians and other scholars studying the Mughal period of Indian history. It is intended to be primarily a reference work. Its scope is therefore modest. Students of Middle Eastern or Central Asian history may detect a number of similarities in the terms, the language, or the positions described in these documents to those found in official documents surviving in their own areas of study. Certainly, a common Mongol heritage and the pan-Islamic Persian administrative tradition are powerful influences for a certain uniformity. I caution against assuming that the Mughal administrative system was simply a transplant diverging little or not at all from other Islamic regimes. The intricate differences between the Ottoman *tīmār* and the Mughal *jāgīr* reveal some of the many distinctions between those imperial administrations.

I wish to thank Professor Sajida Alvi of the Department of South Asian Studies at the University of Minnesota, Minneapolis, for her painstaking reading of my draft typescript of the translation. She has assisted me in arriving at a reasonable rendering of a number of extremely difficult phrases in the text. For this service, and for her encouragement, I am extremely grateful. Dr. Peter Hardy and Dr. Brian Silver have also given the translation a close reading and have made several valuable suggestions. I must record my appreciation to them, Mr. Simon Digby, Dr. Stephen Blake and Dr. N. Gerald Barrier for their enthusiasm for this project and for understanding the importance of these materials in the study of Mughal India. The final responsibility for the work rests with me.

John F. Richards
Durham, North Carolina

Introduction

Between the seventh and seventeenth centuries Muslim generals, kings, adventurers, and *ghāzīs* (warriors for the faith) gradually extended Islamic political and military domination in the Indian subcontinent. Behind this slowly moving frontier line, two processes interlocked. First, the descendants of migrants and converts gradually constituted a specifically Indian, as opposed to an Arabian, Turkish, or Persian, Islamic society. Second, the Indian Muslim state ruling the new society increased its own size, power and wealth, and in the process evolved an increasingly effective, efficient, and internally differentiated bureaucracy. Despite occasional setbacks against the stubborn resistance of indigenous Hindu society, the Muslim state strengthened the confidence and security of the Muslim settlers and their descendants on the subcontinent. By the first quarter of the sixteenth century, just prior to the establishment of the Mughal Empire, Muslim dynasts, political and military elites, and Islamic scholars (the *ᶜulamā'*) solidly controlled states entrenched in the northern and central regions of India. Only the Rajputs, aggressively resurgent in Rajasthan, and the Telugu kingdoms of Vijayanagar, Kondavidu, and Rajkonda offered major resistance to further Muslim expansion.

These centuries of successful state-building and consolidation, based on and supporting an administrative and political tradition, are the background of the present text and its translation. Much of the immense quantity of Persian writing produced in the Indian subcontinent had open political objectives and underlying religious or pious ones. These chronicles, historical narratives, and epic poetry contributed to the elan of Muslim kings or Sultans and their nobles and soldiers and to their sense of identity as conquerors and heroes. Biographical dictionaries of saints, poets, theologians, nobles and generals achieved the same end. Early on, alongside these more visible and more appealing bodies of Indo-Persian writings, the Muslim state produced writing about techniques of military organization and warfare, state administration, and the various arts and crafts essential to a state such as falconry, horsemanship, and farriery, archery, coinage and metallurgy.[1]

By and large, the authors, copyists and students of the more strictly administrative and craft or technical works tended to be lesser or mid-ranking officials employed in bureaucratic positions. They were salaried or subject to a regulated stipend, nonhereditary (formally, at least), and depended on reviews of performance for advancement. These bodies of subordinate officers in the Islamic states were originally nearly exclusively Muslim but increasingly included members of Hindu trading and secretarial castes, Khatris, Kayasthas, and others who learned to speak, read and write fluent Persian, the language of official intercourse.

Without giving up their primary religious affiliation as Hindus, they managed the considerable feat of assimilating to many aspects of Indian Muslim customs and culture outside their homes. They also became steeped in the techniques and regulations and customs of official Indo-Persian routine. Needless to say, given this sort of investment, these men closely identified their prosperity, their honor, and their sense of pride with the fortunes of the states and regimes which they served. By the early 1500s, just as various Hindu warrior aristocrats, Rajputs, Marathas and others were making accommodations and entering the armies of the Indian Muslim regional states, so also were the Hindu secretarial groups becoming official administrators and clerks.

The Emperor Akbar (A.D. 1556–1605) utilized the energy and talents of Rajput warriors in his conquests, and he employed hundreds of assimilated Kayasthas and other Hindu subordinate officials to consolidate and administer those conquests. The growing power and resources of these lower to mid-level officers demanded a technical literature that could be used for instruction and reference in virtually any circumstances. This genre of Mughal Persian writing is usually referred to as the body of "administrative manuals" or the *dastūr al-ᶜamal* writings.[2] The surviving manuscripts (most in several copies) include glossaries and dictionaries of technical administrative terms; instructional tables for the novice first learning the chancery system of numerical notation (*siyāqat*, based on a shorthand version of Arabic words for the numerals); tables for ready reckoning of pay and allowances; copies of imperial regulations and rules; models and samples of official and semi-official letters (copies from the letter books of private secretaries to rulers and officials); sample orders, forms for routine administrative action and finally, model letters of appointment to various official posts.

The original Mughal administrative manual, and still the best known, is the major work by Abul Fazl, the minister of the Emperor Akbar. Abul Fazl's *Āʾīn-i Akbarī* is partly an administrative manual of the type described above, containing texts of appointment orders and regulations for the operation of almost every imperial office and establishment. It also contains a systematic gazetteer describing the various subdistricts, districts and provinces of the late sixteenth century Mughal empire in North India. Abul Fazl completed this massive work as a companion piece for his detailed chronicle of Akbar's reign, the *Akbar-Nāma.*[3] Long available in English translation, the *Āʾīn-i Akbarī* has been and continues to be cited by virtually every writer who makes even passing references to the Mughal empire. Of more interest in the present context, the *Āʾīn-i Akbarī* defined the primary administrative appointments both at the center and within the provinces for the new imperial system, as well as the basic duties, terminology and norms for appointment to those positions. Many of the formulaic duties and exhortations of the present text, written over a century later, originally appeared in the *Āʾīn-i Akbarī.* Abul Fazl's compilation, however, was part of a grand design intended to complete the ideology and structure of an extensive imperial system.[4] Subsequent, far less systematic manuals were far less sweeping and ambitious (see below).

These manuals were reference works, for the secretary who needed to draft a letter of appointment to a provincial fiscal officer in proper form, for instance. They were used for instruction, but instruction was very much a private affair, given and regulated within the family rather than by the regime. To cite one example, the seventeenth century Mughal officer Bhimsen Saxsena, a Kayastha of a North Indian family, first acquired his education and training from the age of seven to fourteen in the city of Aurangabad, "where (he) gained an education and learned the decent manners required in society from his elders." Numerous members of his own family, including his father and uncles, all in Mughal service, tutored him. Bhimsen benefitted as well from the attention and instruction of a superintendent of artillery, Mir Abdul Mabood, a Muslim subordinate to his father, "who used to show his affection and regard in a greater way than to his own sons."[5] Bhimsen obtained his first appointment when he was in his mid-teens, as a protegé of Mir Abdul Mabood: he became an agent (*gumāshta*) to the noble Mirza Raja Jai Singh, a prominent Rajput general under the Emperor Aurangzeb and the former employer of Bhimsen's father. Composing and copying administrative manuals, as Bhimsen had done under the supervision of his mentor, was indispensable, both in providing a professional education and in reinforcing family monopolies of bureaucratic positions, for Muslim and Hindu alike.

This adminstrative tradition continued into the first decades of the eighteenth century until the effective demise of the Mughal empire as a centralized administrative structure (*circa* A.D. 1720–1740). Changes in imperial policy and practices then required revised 'editions' of the manuals and encouraged the writing of new works. After the demise of the imperial system, the copying of these manuals became partly a pious exercise for the descendants of these official families. The Indian servants of the British began to practice the same exercise as the East India Company expanded its control over the subcontinent from A.D. 1750 to 1850. Both of these impulses produced many of the later copies of many Mughal manuals originally written in the seventeenth century.

At present, more than thirty Mughal administrative manuals have been identified, catalogued and utilized (some exist in unique, some in multiple copies).[6] Considering the potential for further discoveries in hitherto unsurveyed and unanalyzed private, local, and even larger public collections of manuscript materials dating from the Mughal period, it seems likely that this number will increase in the future. To date, as far as can be determined, only one such work has been published, in an 1879 lithograph edition from the Nawal Kishore Press in Lucknow.[7] None has been published in translation in English or, apparently, in any Indian language. Perhaps half or more of these manuscripts are available for consultation and study in the major world libraries at Delhi, London, Paris, and Berlin. Others in smaller local collections (some very rich, such as the State Library at Rampur) are not so accessible, either directly or on microfilm.

Aside from difficulties of access, a number of other problems have hindered the use of these works. Many of the existing manuscripts have been copied in either a full or a near-chancery script (*shikasta* or 'broken' writing), making accurate reading often difficult and sometimes impossible. At times it is only possible to read such texts because they also exist in clearly written versions (usually referred to as *nasta*^{c}*līq*, the conventional Indo-Persian hand). Moreover, the eclecticism, absence of explanatory commentary, and lack of discernible organization in many texts, all preclude easy reference to the manuscripts. A major concern is the absence of reliable dating for the regulations and other particulars in the various manuals. As Simon Digby comments in a 1970 review essay:

> Another difficulty lies in the *dastūr al-*^{c}*amals* or manuals of administration which are among the most important sources for these studies. In default of a detailed analysis of the textual traditions of these works, it is extremely difficult to distinguish between information which reflects current conditions (as known to the compiler) from wholesale borrowings from earlier works.[8]

The lack of systematic historical studies of these texts has also handicapped historians' understanding of Mughal administrative terminology, procedures and institutions. In spite of the overwhelming importance of Mughal imperial administrative practices and policies for all aspects of South Asian history after 1550, only now, after nearly a century of historical research, are we beginning to understand this powerful imperial structure. Accurate printed texts and translations of these manuals will help to answer many of the most basic questions in administrative history, such as the administrative domain of a *faujdār* or military governor or definitions of crucial terms.

The present text comprises twenty-five folios or fifty manuscript pages forming a discrete section of the British Museum bound manuscript volume, Oriental 1779.[9] It bears the descriptive heading "List of Contents of Official Appointment Orders (*asnād*) for Positions (filled by) Imperial Servants and for Claimants of Salary Totalling Sixty-Five Orders." Fortunately the Persian text is copied in an elegant, legible and accurate hand running thirteen lines to the manuscript page. The copyist wrote in the conventional Indian Muslim hand instead of the Mughal chancery script. The compiler, although unknown, was almost certainly a Mughal official writing in the reign of the Emperor Bahadur Shah (A.D. 1708–1712) (see below). As the heading suggests, the text, devoid of any sort of expository or connecting matter, includes sixty-five model or sample official warrants; some fifty forms supply the wording for official letters appointing imperial officers or *manṣabdārs* to provincial offices. Several sample letters name local magnates in the countryside or leading merchants in the towns and cities to intermediary offices vital to the

Mughal administrative system. The remaining orders provide texts for recurring, largely routine, fiscal actions such as an officer's claim to receive his salary in cash from the proceeds of market tax revenues.[10]

That these are sample or model orders is clear from the absence of proper names in all save a few orders. The compiler has instead followed the custom of substituting the term *fulān*, meaning undesignated, for the name of the official appointee, or for the subdistrict or other administrative unit and for the date. The translation has rendered this term simply as a blank line: "the position is conferred upon ______"; " of ______ subdistrict," and so forth (the translation treats the period of appointment, and amounts of tribute, in the same way). Even a cursory examination of the text suggests that the compiler intended it as a reference work or manual for clerks in the imperial chancery, charged with drafting letters of appointment. As we have suggested above, the text could also have been utilized to train youths in apprenticeship, either within the family or as junior assistants in the imperial offices.

The compiler of the text remains anonymous, although internal evidence suggests that he was probably an official within the Mughal fiscal administration, possibly at the provincial level during the last years of the reign of the Emperor Aurangzeb (ruled A.D. 1658–1707). He evidently remained active during the first decade of the eighteenth century. The sixty-five orders he selected for this collection were almost certainly in current use in the last decade of Aurangzeb's reign (A.D. 1697–1707) and as late as the end of the reign of the latter's son and immediate successor Bahadur Shah (1708–1712). The phrase "from among the arrears and revenue advances dating from the forty-second regnal year of the *Ḥaẓrat Khuld Makānī*" appears in the text of three of the *asnād* of appointment – that for the chief provincial fiscal officer or *dīwān*, (folio 216b), for the district executive and revenue officer, the *faujdār* and *amīn* (217b) and the subdistrict revenue collector, the *karōṛī* (folio 219a). This phrase is the posthumous title of the Emperor Aurangzeb. Therefore, the text of the orders of appointment, the normative injunctions, and the configuration of official positions and duties in these forms probably originated in the late Mughal period, at the turn of the eighteenth century. In other words, these documents are most likely to reflect Mughal official structures after well over a century of change and imperial territorial expansion. Growing political and fiscal pressures on the system from the Deccan wars and the Maratha resurgence had not yet substantially altered this system in practice. The first definitive evidence of serious and prolonged breakdown in the system appears in the reign of the Emperor Farrukhsiyar (1713–1719).

What then are the official posts for which these model letters of appointment were intended? Fifty-five of the orders compiled set out the proper wording and form for appointment to a total of sixty offices (several letters can be used for more than one similar post). The appointments mentioned in this collection range from that of provincial governor (the *ṣūbadār*, 215b), deputy governor, chief provincial fiscal officer (*dīwān*, folio 217a), city magistrates (*kotwāl*, folio 224a), and others of the most prominent official posts found within an imperial province, to lesser officials such as subdistrict treasurers (folio 219b), accountants, news reporters, and writers of receipts. No rigid order appears in the arrangement of these form letters by the compiler, but he has generally placed the most important offices in the first half of the collection, before the lesser or subordinate offices.[11] The texts for the higher posts are much more explicit, and replete with honorific phrases and exhortations for proper behavior. Those for the subordinate posts tend toward the terse and laconic. Whether long or short, each patent of office follows a uniform formula. After the heading naming the title of the office, the next section sets out: the position once again; its location in a subdistrict (*pargana*), district (*sarkār*), province (*ṣūba*), city (*balda*), or port (*bandar*); the name of the officer removed and the name of the officer appointed; and possibly the date. Then follows the unchanging exhortation that the appointee "must fulfill the duties and customary obligations of that position with rectitude and propriety." Next, in the longer texts, we find a general statement of responsibility such as to promote agriculture, nurture peasantry, etc. The actual duties of the office are set out in the very next passage, which may be extensive or brief. Finally the patent of office terminates with a general order directed to those imperial officials and nonofficial groups who may be expected to have some dealings with the appointee to accept and to respect his legitimate authority.

The only significant variation in this formula lies in the introductory section. For the higher-ranking offices, the phrase translated "according to the exalted order" (*ḥasbu'l ḥukm-i ʿalā*) precedes the sentence detailing the appointment's location and the names of its incumbents. For the remaining subordinate officers, approximately two-thirds of the total, the model orders commence abruptly with the phrase: "This order (*dastak*) is issued to (literally, 'in the names of') the responsible officers, etc." Apparently, this terminological distinction reflects a difference in the appointing authority: for the higher offices, the act of authorization and approval emanated from the central administration in the office of the *wazīr* or head *dīwān* of the empire. For the subordinate offices the appointing authority issuing the order was probably the provincial *dīwān*. In either case, it is certain that nearly all the posts included in this collection were to be filled by free officers already engaged in imperial service (as the use of the term *taghīr*, "transferred", implies). The appointees would thus have been *manṣabdārs* or rank-holders whose status, pay and official responsibilities were determined by possession of a personal rank expressed in numerical, decimal figures, from 20 *ẓāt* to as high as 5000 *ẓāt*. As the repository of all legitimate authority, precedence and honor in the official system, the Emperor ultimately either set or approved *ẓāt* rank.[12] At most, five or six of these positions were to be filled by non-*manṣabdārs*, such as a local notable or aristocrat awarded a semiheriditary, collaborative position as headman or *chaudhurī* of a subdistrict (see below).

A close scrutiny of these official posts reveals a number of significant omissions. For example, no orders appear for the canonical/judicial offices of an Islamic state common to Indian Muslim regimes. We know that the Mughals employed provincial *qāẓīs* or judges. They designated *qāẓīs*, drawn from the ranks of Muslim scholars or *ʿulamā'*, for every town (*qaṣaba*) serving as the headquarters of a subdistrict, and for larger towns and cities.[13] We know that in A.D. 1659 the Emperor Aurangzeb revived the office of *muḥtasib* (usually mistranslated as censor) and placed these officers under the control of judges throughout the empire to enforce prohibitions against wine drinking, apostasy, and blasphemy and to assist in the regulation of markets and commerce.[14] Similarly, no order is included for the provincial *ṣadr* or "almoner" in charge of regulating state grants to worthy, usually religious recipients. On the military/executive side, we find no warrant for the provincial *bakhshī*, or chief military inspection officer in charge of certifying *manṣabdārs* for receipt of either direct pay or salary assignments (*jāgīrs*). Finally, warrants for the commander or *qilʿadār* of major fortresses assigned under a direct and independent authorization from the Emperor, are absent. In short, despite first appearances, this is far from a complete collection of orders for all official posts within a Mughal province.

What then does this compilation represent? Essentially, it appears to have been the text of orders for all provincial offices appointed by and subject to partial or full control by the central *dīwān* or *wazīr* of the Empire. It is probable that the actual orders of appointment issued from the second imperial *dīwān*, the *dīwān-i khāliṣa sharīf*, who was in charge of the reserved or centrally administered lands of the empire[15] and of all revenues to come directly into the central imperial treasury. The *dīwān-i khālisạ sharīf's* duties included the appointment of officials. Thus, the phrase "in accordance with the exalted order" probably refers to the command of the Emperor transmitted through the imperial *wazīr* to the second *dīwān*. For subordinate posts, the *dastaks*, as suggested above, probably issued from the office of the provincial *dīwān* rather than directly from the *dīwān* of the *khāliṣa*. Whether these appointments and transfers were subject to previous scrutiny from the center is uncertain. The anonymous compiler in this case apparently aimed to provide his colleagues, successors and/or pupils with a complete guide to the letters of appointment for virtually all official appointments made by the imperial *dīwān* or *wazīr* and the *dīwān-i khāliṣa*. To have the necessary technical knowledge and experience, the compiler must have served in a clerical or even a higher-status position in that central office. In other words, this compilation of sixty-odd appointment forms was a reference manual for use in the central fiscal and administrative organization of the empire. Only incidentally does it detail the majority of official positions in an imperial province in the late seventeenth and early eighteenth century.

As mentioned above, the texts supplied do not include orders for posts falling under other central ministers and offices. Thus, the imperial *ṣadr* and chief *qāẓī* assigned men learned in the *sharīʿa* to vacancies for judges, *muḥtasibs*, preachers, etc. The imperial inspector-general, the chief *bakhshī*, sent his own subordinates to the provincial military contingents. The Emperor himself directly appointed the most reliable *manṣabdārs* as fortress commanders.

The *dīwān*, however, seems to have made the great majority of provincial appointments. The *dīwān* also recruited, appointed, supervised and monitored the occupants of the semiofficial or intermediary posts found in each province. Those represented in this compilation include the following: the *chaudhurī* (folio 220a), usually a member of a local warrior caste and dominant head of a stratified lineage. The *chaudhurī* ruled a locality, either one or more subdistricts of as many as one hundred contiguous peasant and craft villages, the *pargana*, or a portion of a larger *pargana*, called a *ṭappā*.[16] The imperial *dīwān* and the *dīwān-i khāliṣa* also appointed or confirmed the appointment of a *chaudhurī* for each province. The latter was drawn from one of the more powerful local aristocratic houses and lineages of the region. Firmly identified with the imperial regime, the *chaudhurī* was supposed to assist all imperial officers sent to his locality in keeping order, filing reports, etc. He was particularly responsible for collecting revenues, and he could find himself under considerable pressure to make up any accumulated arrears. In return for these services, the weight of state power and authority supported his personal power against recalcitrant kinsmen or other challenges to his local position. He received further returns in the form of tax-exempt lands and a fixed allowance of up to five percent on the revenues collected yearly.

The *dīwān* of the empire also recognized the local power and resources of numerous local magnates by formally designating them as *zamīndārs*. Those *zamīndārs* whose domains were situated within the zone of direct imperial administration (as opposed to the tributary *rājās* given the same label by the Mughals) maintained a relationship with the imperial administration very similar to that of the *chaudhurīs*, in mediating between the state on one side and both rural and town society on the other. The Mughals considered *zamīndār* the generic term, and *chaudhurī* a special office awarded to certain favored local warrior-aristocrats. However, the *zamīndār's* territorial responsibility, unlike that of the *chaudhurī*, extended only to those lands from which he had the prescriptive, hereditary right to levy labor (for military service) and agricultural produce. The *zamīndār's* domain was not tied to an administrative unit, but varied considerably in size. Accordingly, the number of *zamīndārs* incorporated into the Mughal system was considerably greater than those *chaudhurīs* named for each subdistrict and province.

In contrast to the orders set out for posts filled by imperial *manṣabdārs*, newly designated *chaudhurīs* and *zamīndārs* had to make a monetary payment called *peshkash*, the term used for tribute in the Indian Muslim political system. The text of a letter of official "appointment" to an imperial office or status reflected the responsibilities and duties clearly understood by all concerned. At the same time, the *sanad* or order of appointment for each *zamīndār* also reflected diplomatic negotiation and political submission. The incumbents of these offices, although subject to dismissal, were certainly not *manṣabdārs* or full-time servants of the empire. They could be removed from their ancestral lands, or stripped of their command of armed retainers, only by force. Only occasionally, on a temporary basis, could the *chaudhurīs* and *zamīndārs* be mobilized to sustain order against the threat of rebellion or external invasion. The occupants of these posts also anticipated that their descendants would continue to occupy these posts in return for loyal service, in contrast to the anti-hereditary Mughal posting of *manṣabdārs* to offices. Continuing administrative consolidation and enhanced imperial efficiency during the seventeenth century, however, meant that many members of this class found themselves under steady pressure from the empire. More and more, they resembled fully-fledged officials dependent on the central state, rather than autonomous and proud local magnates.

Two other less powerful figures also came under the jurisdiction of the *dīwān's* office. The local record-keeper and accountant, or *qānūngo*, working in tandem with the *chaudhurī*, served the empire in every subdistrict. Generally, occupants of these positions were recruited from the literate secretarial castes such as Khatris or Brahmins. They seldom had the resources or local status of the warrior-aristocrats, who became *chaudhurīs*, and could bargain far less effectively with the imperial administration. Nonetheless, by controlling data on the revenue system, and by accruing wealth over time, the subdistrict *qānūngos* became important local figures in the seventeenth century. Their terms of employment and conditions of tenure were similar to those of the *chaudhurī* though somewhat less lucrative: they received tax-exempt grants of a small percentage on the revenue proceeds, and other perquisites. The subdistrict accountants paid a fixed amount of *peshkash* on the same terms as the *chaudhurī*.

Finally, the headman (*chaudhurī*, folio 223b) of the *sā'ir* revenues assumed responsibility for proper management and taxing of town and urban markets. The order of appointment of *dastak* incorporated in our text requires an appointee to pay a fixed fee, (not termed *peshkash*) in order to occupy the post. Most, if not all, of these *sā'ir* headmen were either bankers, money changers or prominent merchants of the town or city in which the post was located. They were placed between the Mughal *manṣabdārs* serving in the *sā'ir* administration (the superintendent and assessor of these revenues, the accountant, etc.) and the corporate bodies of traders, merchants, and artisans. These headmen provided an important link between the local and central administrations, and a means for controlling urban commerce for the regime. The provincial *dīwān* also seems to have designated or at least approved a headman for each of the discrete urban markets. These headmen necessarily worked in close conjunction with the headman of the *sā'ir* revenues.

Before discussing each group of offices in turn, it is essential to look first at the administrative levels which emerge from a close study of these sixty-odd forms of appointment. As mentioned above, the usual territorial/administrative sequence cited is that used by the Mughals themselves, beginning with the peasant village and moving upward to the subdistrict (ten to a hundred villages), the district or *sarkār* (several hundred or even a thousand villages), and the province or *ṣūba* (several thousand towns and villages). Generally, the Mughal province was a distinct linguistic cultural region (e.g., Gujarat) frequently ruled by a single dynasty or state prior to the sixteenth century and resembling similar proto-national linguistic and cultural regions in Europe or China. By contrast, as mentioned earlier, the *pargana* or subdistrict was a compact, county-sized unit in which a stratified lineage of warrior-aristocrats ruled by force and customary right. At times headed by a petty *rājā* or chief, at times by a group of dominant leading members, the elite of these stratified lineages controlled, when necessary by force, the peasant villages of the *pargana.* The appurtenances of state power – although on a small scale – concentrated in the *pargana* town (*qaṣaba*), which was the headquarters of the lineage. The subdistrict or *pargana*, not the individual village, was the primary unit of rural social and political control for all Indian Muslim regimes, including the Mughal. Similarly, at the other end of the scale, the province or *ṣūba* (there were over twenty by the mid-seventeenth century) was the largest imperial unit. Invariably, when formerly independent Sultanates or Hindu kingdoms were forcibly assimilated to the regulation imperial system, the boundaries of the kingdom remained intact to serve as provincial boundaries. On the local level, subdistrict boundaries and names seem to have changed very rarely.[17]

What then of the district or *sarkār*? Judging by this particular collection, the district remained little more than a formal, artificial unit for the imperial sytem. Throughout the empire, districts seem to have been the former provinces of those states conquered by the Mughal armies. Names and boundaries remained unaltered, but we do not find any body of officials appointed at the district level whose jurisdictions coincided with the territory of a district. Official documents mention districts for purposes of location and identification, and list district revenue valuations, but little else. Instead the Mughals relied upon a more flexible, versatile form of intermediate administration lying between the local unit and the region. This was the *faujdārī* or territorial jurisdiction of a single *faujdār.* Often cutting across district boundaries (but never across provincial or *pargana* lines), the jurisdiction of an individual *faujdār* reflected the perceived need of the center for more or less intensive control and surveillance. Thus different degrees of cooperation or resistance among the local *zamīndārs*, or differences in terrain helped to determine the extent of territory assigned to a *faujdār.*[18] As we can readily see by the first part of the assignment order reproduced below for the *faujdār*, the office demanded active, interventionist occupants. Commanding several hundred armed heavy cavalry, the *faujdār* was a visible and formidable reminder of imperial power in the countryside throughout the Mughal empire. Moreover, the *faujdār* supervised a net of commanders of military checkpoints (*thānadārs*) and a number of commanders of road patrols (*rāhdārs*) (see figure 2). A dozen or more strategic castles, commanded by independently commissioned officers (*qilʿadār*) and substantially garrisoned by Mughal troops, completed the display of imperial power within each province. In short, the key elements in Mughal provincial administration include the clustering of offices at the provincial and subdistrict levels (within the basic indigenous units of local society); the use of the *faujdār* as a flexible intermediate instrument whose military and executive responsibilities varied according to local conditions; and finally the ultimate safeguard of fortified strongpoints distributed throughout the province.

To conclude this brief introduction, it may be helpful to set out schematically the primary functional relationships among and between these imperial offices. The appended organizational charts (figures 2 through 6) sketch the lines of hierarchy, by placing subordinate offices directly beneath and/or adjacent to superior offices and the types of responsibilities attributed to each office. The imperial posts whose forms of appointment are incorporated in this collection, fall into five functional groupings, according to the duties and jurisdiction of the individual office. The five groups illustrated in the figure are: executive and military offices; offices for fiscal and monetary control; land tax management and collection offices; urban administration offices (for cities and ports); and urban revenue offices. These categories are not necessarily drawn from or congruent with the imperial Mughal taxonomy. Nor are they identical with conventions in present-day scholarly discussions of the imperial administration, which are drawn largely from the original Mughal categories. However, this new schema may help to clarify a very complex administrative system, without doing violence to any of the established taxonomies.

The absence of any district officers is evident in the executive military grouping (figure 2). The gathering and reporting of public events and secret intelligence is assigned (as most writers on Mughal administration note) both to the newswriter posted in subdistrict towns and to the superintendents of the post. This collection of document forms does not include the office of provincial *bakhshī* and his subordinates.

The offices for fiscal and monetary control at the provincial level can be seen to break down into four distinct units (figure 3), all under the direct supervision and control of the provincial *dīwān*. The functions of the provincial treasury offices are self-explanatory. The provincial mint employed four senior officers, whose titles largely explained their functions. Finally, grouping the auditor of accounts, the claims settlement officer and the receipt writer together suggests the imperial administration's care to control expenditures and transfers of funds, and to prevent leakages. All such transactions were followed by a paper trail of vouchers, receipts, certificates, countervailing signatures and seals.

The imperial administration devoted its largest single nonmilitary administrative effort to the management and collection of the land tax (figure 4). Thus it is scarcely surprising that the terminology, the offices, and the operations of this part of the imperial system are extremely difficult to comprehend. The complexity of the system and the many unresolved issues of interpretation make it difficult to summarize the system. However, the Mughal land tax basically represented a royal prescriptive claim upon the product of the land, expressed as a fraction of from one-ninth to as much as one-half of that product under the later Mughal emperors. The Mughal system stated the tax as a uniform assessed rate for areas of relatively uniform crop, soil, and climate conditions. This assessment was revised annually by a rolling ten-year average figure for production based upon annual yields per crop and average market prices per crop. The assessed tax was expressed in money and collected insofar as possible completely in cash. This system forced the sale of food grains and other agrarian products on the market. The peasantry and their overlords, the *zamīndārs*, brought those foodstuffs into the cities to obtain cash with which to pay the land tax demand in the proper installments. The basic units of assessment and collection were the villages, whose fields were measured and crops noted at periodic intervals.

The land tax management offices included in the text are set out in figure 4. The principal executive in the system was the *dīwān* of the province. He was primarily responsible for ensuring proper assessment and collection of the land revenue by all official and quasi-official persons involved in the system. The *dīwān* was also expected to extend cultivation by giving loans or tax reductions to persons breaking in new or waste lands. The *dīwān* was required to monitor and expedite the flow of cash generated by this system from the *pargana* treasuries to the imperial coffers at the capital or the Emperor's camp.

The schematic outline places immediately beneath the *dīwān* two officers of roughly equivalent status and functions: the *amīn* of *pāybāqī* and the *amīn* of all other remaining lands. These two officers and their staffs set the current assessment for villages and *parganas* in the province based upon the rolling ten-year average yield and market figures per crop and per unit of area. Categories *a* and *b*, the lands held temporarily and the centrally reserved tracts, fell under the direct responsibility of the *dīwān's* office for both assessment and collection of revenues. Category *c* or *jāgīr* lands, were subject to assessment and valuation by the *dīwān's* office, but not to collection. The latter was the function of the privately employed agent to the assignment holder, an imperial officer formally given those lands to meet the salaries of himself and his followers. This organization thus used three types of revenue collectors: those in category *a* under the supervision of the *amīn* of *pāybāqī*; those in category *b* under the *amīn* (for *khāliṣa sharīf* lands); and in category *c* the agents of the *jāgīrdārs*. Whether as officials or agents, the collectors seem to have been present in virtually all *parganas* or subdistricts. Under the *dīwān* or the *amīn* of the *pargana* a subordinate official, also called an *amīn,* may have served in each *pargana* as well. In this text, however, we do not find a warrant for such an officer.[19] A small group of subordinate officials including the treasurer, accountant (*mushrif*), a collector (*ᶜāmil*), a transmittal officer, and possibly an assessor or manager (*amīn*) were probably placed in every *pargana* or perhaps grouping of *parganas.*

Figure 5 outlines the offices for general urban administration found in this compilation. The central figure here is the city magistrate or *kotwāl,* who acted with the *qāẓī* or judge and with the commander of the city's citadel or fortress in assuming overall responsibility for the peace, order and security of the city or town and its immediate environs. Naturally, the *kotwāl's* duties and his stature were somewhat reduced at the provincial capital serving as the seat of the imperial governor. Elsewhere, he was a most important figure. His city guards and watchmen and various other bodies of armed footmen were the urban police. He, more than any other officer, was responsible for controlling the urban crowd and for mitigating and subduing the sectarian violence that could break out rapidly in the seventeenth century Indian urban environment. If the city were a seaport as well, an additional cluster of officials collected ships' duties and customs; maintained the docking and harbor facilities; and provided security for traders and their goods, sea captains and their ships. The imperial flotilla of war-boats, usually shallow-draft riverine or coastal vessels, armed and equipped with oars and sails, was based in the major ports. The *mīr baḥr* and his staff commanded and maintained this flotilla with its contingents of sailors and gunners against local pirates and rebels. Finally at the seaports the superintendent of the salt pans was in charge of the highly lucrative state monopoly of sea-salt. The precise relationship between the port administrator or *mutaṣaddī* and the city magistrate is not yet clear. The magistrate may well have been subordinate to the port administrator who, in the case of Surat at least, was treated as a high-ranking and highly responsible official.

The urban revenue offices illustrated in figure 6 included three sets of positions. First, the manager or executive (*amīn*) of these revenues supervised a sizeable staff. His senior officers included a superintendent of his office, an appraiser who valued goods for customs purposes, a cashier and an accountant. The *amīn* had jurisdiction over various markets for commodities and services within the city. The imperial administration considered each a fiscal unit, or *maḥal.* Second, Mughal officers of subordinate rank, also called *amīns*, supervised each *maḥal.* In conjunction with them, local headmen or *chaudhurīs* served in each market. As the term implies, these were prominent local merchants or bankers. The *amīn* of *sā'ir* also exercised authority over the inland customs posts at each town and along major road and water routes in the province. None of these posts, however, are incorporated in this text.

Notes

1 *See* the articles "Inshā'" and "Diplomatic" in the *Encyclopaedia of Islam,* second edition, revised, for general treatments of the evolution of official

forms of documents and correspondence in Arabic, Persian and Turkish. In general, Mughal forms and terminology, written uniformly in Persian (with occasional bilingual documents in Persian/Hindi or Persian/Marathi) were similar to contemporary Safavid Persian forms. Byzantine administrative practices apparently heavily influenced the Ottoman practices. For a sample of Safavid terms and administrative institutions, *see* V. Minorsky, *Tadhkirat al-Mulūk*, London, the E. J. W. Gibb Memorial Series, n.s. XVI (London, 1943). Dated at *circa* A.D. 1725, this manual represents the mature Safavid administrative structure and style. A close comparison of the present text with the *Tadhkirat al-Mulūk* will reveal many superficially similar terms and offices, but larger and very wide divergences in areas such as salary assignment, management of royal crown lands, appointment of nobles, and military organization.

2 Irfan Habib, in *The Agrarian System of Mughal India* (Aligarh, 1963), p. 202n, translates *dastūr al-ᶜamal* in this context as "regulations guiding executive work." More narrowly, the term can mean schedules of cash revenue rates. Historians now use the term to refer generally to any sort of Mughal normative manual or compilation surviving from the sixteenth to the eighteenth centuries. Sri Ram Sharma, *A Bibliography of Mughal India, A.D. 1526–1707* (Bombay, n.d.), chap. 10, "Administrative Manuals," pp. 107–128, lists the full contents of ten of the better known works. Sharma does not include the present text (British Museum, Oriental 1779) in his bibliography.

One of the most complete collections of official warrants of appointment occurs in a manuscript in the Bodleian Library. Persian e-l, the *Nigārnāma-i Munshī* by "Malikzāda," dated about A.D. 1684, contains a number of letters of appointment for offices included in this text. The language is virtually identical, with only very slight changes in some honorifics. For examples, see the *amīn* of *sā'ir's* appointment order (folios 142b and 143a), or that of the city *kotwāl* (folios 145b–146a) and the *dīwān* of the army (folio 146a). The Bodleian manuscript offers a wider range of appointments made by other officers such as the *bakhshī* (military executive officer) as well as those made by the *dīwān* of the *khāliṣa.*

3 Abul Fazl's *Ā'īn-i Akbarī*, translated by Blockman and Jarrett, was originally published by the Royal Asiatic Society of Bengal, Calcutta, in three volumes, 1873–96. Later revisions of the translation were published in 1939 (vol. 1) and 1948–49 (vols. 2 and 3). The *Akbar- Nāma* of Abul Fazl, translated by Henry Beveridge, was published from Calcutta by the Royal Asiatic Society of Bengal in three volumes, 1897–1921.

4 See J. F. Richards, "The Formulation of Imperial Authority Under Akbar and Jahangir," in J. F. Richards, ed., *Kingship and Authority in South Asia* (Madison, Wisconsin, 1978), for the role played by the *Akbar-Nāma* in Abul Fazl's attempt to construct a viable dynastic ideology. On the construction of the administrative system, see Irfan Habib, *The Agrarian System*, and I. H. Qureshi, *The Administration of the Mughul Empire*, (Karachi, 1966).

5 Bhimsen Saxsena, *Tarikh-i Dilkusha*, edited by V. G. Khobrekar, translation by Khobrekar and Jadunath Sarkar (Bombay, 1972), pp. 62–65. The first portion of Bhimsen's memoir, (folios 1–104), entitled the *Tarīkh-i Dilkushā*, has survived in a manuscript now in the collection of the India Office Library (Ethe, 445; Mss. 94); the second, entitled *Nuskha-i Dilkushā* (folios 95–158), is extant in a British Museum Persian manuscript (Oriental 23; Rieu, I, 271). I possess a filmed copy of the second portion of the manuscript, but not the

first. Therefore I have not been able to verify the translation against the text.

6 Irfan Habib offers the most comprehensive listing of these manuals yet attempted. In *The Agrarian System*, pp. 412–413, he cites twenty-five works, provides brief descriptive comments, and dates each manual approximately.

7 Cf. Habib, *The Agrarian System*: "In view of the great importance of these works as sources of administrative and revenue history, it is certainly a pity that none of them has been printed so far, except for [the *Siyāqnāma* of Munshi Nand Rām] which was printed some eighty years ago" (p. 412).

8 Simon Digby, review of N. A. Siddiqui, *Land Revenue Administration Under the Mughals 1700–1975* (London, 1970), in University of London, *Bulletin of the School of Oriental and African Studies*, 34(1971): 418.

9 In his catalogue of the *Persian Manuscripts of the British Museum* (London, 1966 reprint) Charles Rieu lists this volume under the title "Manuscripts of Mixed Contents," and simply notes that, "apparently [written] in the 18th century," the work contains "revenue tables of the Ṣūbahs and Parganahs in the reigns of Shāhjahān and Aurangzib, with forms of appointment to various offices" (Rieu, III, 990). The British Museum received the volume from the son of Sir Henry Elliot in 1875. Henry Elliot senior, a British Indian official, was one of the first scholars to systematically search out, collect, and publish Persian chronicles and documents from the entire Indian Muslim period. His eight-volume compendium of translated excerpts from Indo-Muslim Persian writings is still a standard reference: H. M. Elliot and John Dowson, eds., *The History of India As Told By Its Own Historians* (eight volumes, 1964 reprint edition). Another copy of the Oriental 1779 text survives in the British Museum manuscript Oriental 1842. This manuscript volume seems to be a later collection made for a British official, possibly in the nineteenth century. The text in Oriental 1842 (folios 99–137) is identical to that of the sixty-five forms of appointment set out in Oriental 1779. Only the title differs slightly: "Contents of Official Appointment Orders According to the Exalted Office (*daftar-vālā*)." *Cf. Rieu, III, 1030.*

10 Surprisingly enough, only one historian writing on Mughal administration has made extensive or systematic use of these texts. In his study of Mughal administration, I. H. Qureshi refers frequently to this compendium of orders in his chapter on provincial administration. See I. H. Qureshi, *The Administration of the Mughul Empire*, pp. 227–247. Qureshi lists the work as *Kaifiyat-i ṣūbajāt-i-mumālik-i-maḥrusah-i-Hindūstān* (for the entire volume), and cites other portions of the manuscript as well.

11 In *The Chancellery and Persian Epistolography Under the Mughals* (Calcutta, 1971), Momin Mohiuddin distinguishes two types of appointment letters in his discussion of the routine papers generated in the Mughal administrative system, as opposed to the special orders issued by the Emperor and his chief ministers (pp. 95–97): "All appointments to higher posts at the Capital and provinces (for example to the post of a *nāẓim* or the provincial governor . . . were made by the Emperor himself in the "*farmān-i-ẓabtī*: whereas all other appointments to district and *pargana* posts were made" by the ministers in their respective departments, but with the approval of the *dīvān-i-aʿlā*, in the *ḥasb al-ḥukm letters patent*." On the other hand, lesser appointments were made by routine voucher or *dastak*: "Certain appointments to minor posts in the parganas and the ministries were made by the . . . *letters patent* called the *dastakāt-i-khidmāt* for the posts of *dārūgha*, *taḥvildār*, and *mushrifs* . . . . In each case the written order of the vizier was necessary."

12 Consult M. Athar Ali, *The Mughal Nobility under Aurangzeb* (Aligarh, 1966), pp. 7–11, 38–72, for further information on the ranked and graded imperial cadre of civil and military officers. Each *manṣabdār*, depending upon his personal rank and his trooper or *suwār* rank (also expressed decimally), headed a cluster of men who also served the empire and in fact far outnumbered the perhaps eight to ten thousand *manṣabdārs*. Thus the Emperor, the princes, all nobles (*manṣabdārs* bearing a personal or *ẓāt* rank over one thousand), and all lesser members of the cadre employed, paid, managed and commanded persons in their private service. These retinues ranged from as few as two or three men to as many as five thousand for the great nobles. These employees were military officers, administrators, clerks, secretaries, treasurers, physicians, artists, cavalry troopers, domestic servants and menials of all sorts, or slaves (usually eunuchs if male). As we might expect, various kinsmen and lineage-mates formed the core of these 'clusters'. Another large cadre of mounted military men, the *aḥadīyān* or *aḥadīs*, served the Emperor directly as individual bodyguards, messengers, etc. These were not *manṣabdārs* per se since they did not hold decimal ranks, but they seem to have shared many of the social attributes and origins of the *manṣabdārs*. Neither officers and men in private service nor *aḥadīs* filled offices of the type described by the form letters in the present text.

13 See Zameeruddin Siddiqi, "The Institution of the Qazi Under the Mughals," *Medieval Miscellany*, 1 (1969): 240–259, for an excellent discussion of the duties and functioning of the *qāẓī* within the Mughal administration.

14 See Muhammad Zamiruddin Siddiqi, "The Muhtasib Under Aurangzeb," *Medieval India Quarterly*, 5 (1963): 113–119, for a detailed treatment of this office under the Emperor Aurangzeb.

15 Sarkar, *Mughal Administration* (Calcutta, 4th edition, 1952), p. 35.

16 See Richard G. Fox, *Kin, Clan, Raja and Rule* (Berkeley, 1971), pp. 17–47 on the *pargana* as a local sociopolitical unit dominated by one or more stratified lineages.

17 This was unquestionably true for the last great conquest of the empire in the south in 1687–88. The *parganas* and provinces of the kingdom of Golconda retained their original names and boundaries when incorporated into the empire. See Richards, *Mughal Administration in Golconda* (Oxford, 1975), pp. 99–100.

18 See Noman Ahmad Siddiqi, "The *Faujdār* and *Faujdārī* under the Mughals," *Medieval India Quarterly*, 4 (1961): 22–35, for a definitive discussion of the jurisdiction and duties of a *faujdār*. His conclusions have been amply confirmed by more recent provincial studies. See Anjali Chatterjee, *Bengal in the Reign of Aurangzib, 1658–1707* (Calcutta, 1967), pp. 39–45.

19 Scholars have yet to settle this question. Ibn Hasan, for example, in *The Central Structure of the Mughal Empire* (Karachi, 1967, reprint ed.), p. 368, reproduced an order for appointment for an *amīn* of the *pargana* of *Raḥīmābād*, Lucknow district, Anadh (Oudh) province. Although this seems straightforward enough, the text does refer (line 4) to different *maḥals*, plural, in his jurisdiction. The term *maḥal*, of course, is ambiguous and can mean either a *pargana* as a revenue unit or another type of fiscal unit.

Figure One

Administrative Divisions

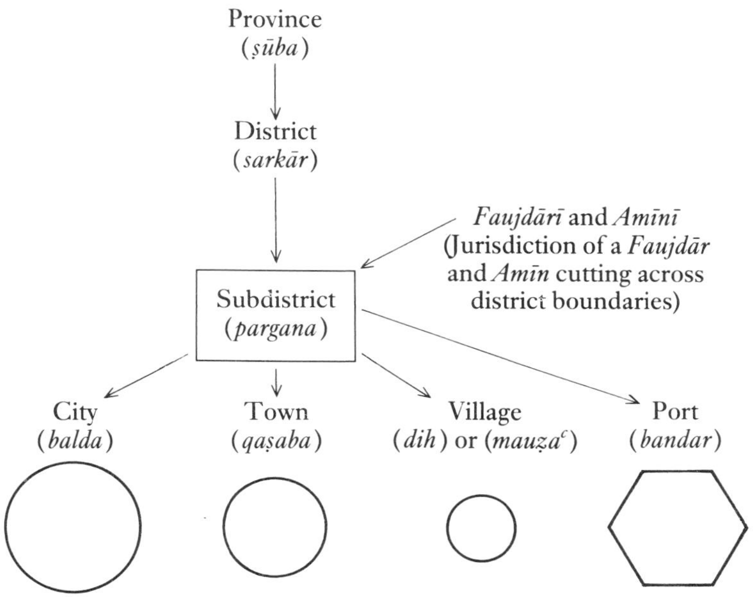

Figure Two

Executive Posts

PROVINCE	Governor (*ṣūbadār*)	
	Deputy Governor (*nā'ib nāẓim*)	
DISTRICT	*Faujdār*	*Faujdār* of a *Jāgīr*
	Military Post Commander (*thānadār*)	
	Highway Security Commander (*rāhdār*)	
SUBDISTRICT	Headman of a Subdistrict(s) (*chaudhurī*)	
Newswriter (*akhbār-nawīs*)		
		Local Magnate (*zamīndār*)
	Village Headman (not given)	

Figure Three

Dīwān of the Province

Treasury

Superintendent
(*dārogha*)

Transmittal Officer
(*sazāwal*)

Receipt Writer for *Manṣabdārs*
(*qabẓ-nawīsī manṣabdārān*)

Fiscal Control

Auditor of Accounts
(*barāmad-nawīs*)

Claims Settlement
(*istīfā'*)

Mint

Superintendent and Head
(*dārogha wa amīn*)

Assay-Master
(*ṣāḥib-ᶜiyār*)

Assayer and Weigh-Master
(*chaukasī wa wazn-kash*)

Army

Finance Officer of the Army
(*dīwān-i fauj*)

Secretary to the Finance Officer
(*peshkār*)

Fiscal Control and Monetary Offices

Figure Four

Land Tax Management and Collection Offices

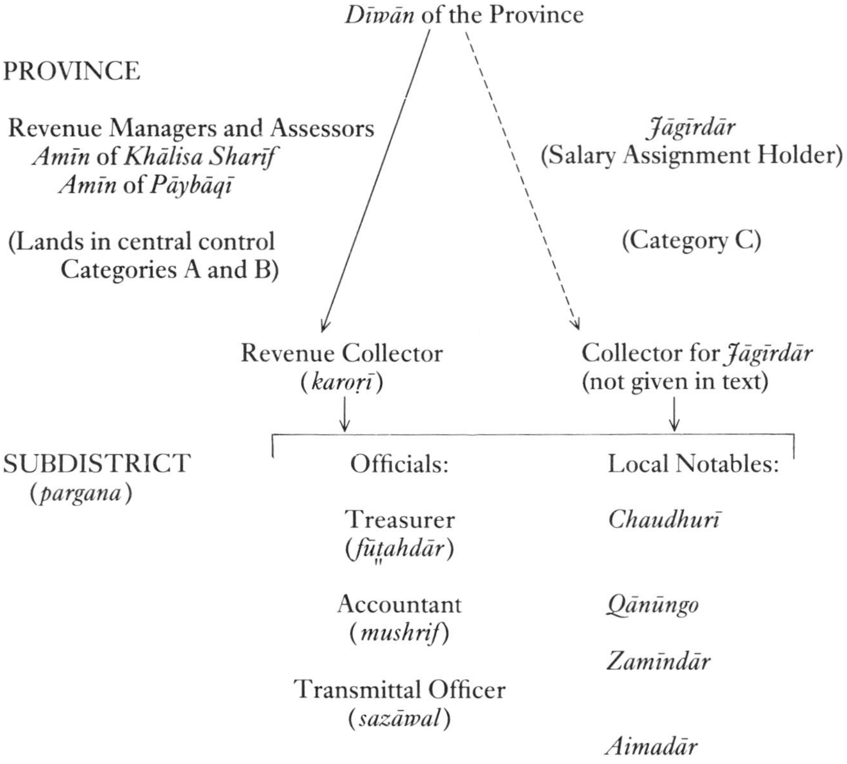

Figure Five

Deputy Governor (*nā'ib nāẓim*)

City (*balda*)

City Magistrate (*kotwāl*)

Manager of the Magistrate's Office (*amīn-i chabūtara kotwāl-i balda*)

Record Keeper of the Magistrate's Goal (*mushrif*)

Commanders of Footmen and Bailiffs (*mīr-dah; mīr-dandī; mīr-nāẓir*)

Judge (not given) (*qaẓī*)

Muḥtasib (not given)

Port (*bandar*)

Port Administrator (*mutaṣaddī*)

Commander of War-Boats (*mīr-baḥrī-i nawāra*)

Superintendent of War-Boats (*dārogha-i nawāra*)

Master of the Docks (*mīr bandar-i furẓat*)

Supervisor of Ships (*dārogha-i jahāzāt*)

Captain of Ships (*nākhudā'ī jahāzāt*)

Superintendent of the Salt Pans (*dārogha-i namaksār bandar*)

Offices of Urban Administration

Figure Six

Urban Revenue Offices

CITY OFFICIALS

Manager and Head for Units of *Sā'ir* Revenues
(*amīn*)

LOCAL NOTABLES

Superintendent
(*dārogha*)

* Headman for Units of
the *Sā'ir* Revenues
(*chaudhurī*)

Cashkeeper
(*taḥwīldār*)

Accountant
(*mushrif*)

Superintentent of Grain Sales
(*dārogha-i mubīʿi ghallāt*)

Markets (*maḥals*)

* Headman of the Money-Changers' Market
(*chaudhurī-i ṣarrāfat*)

Manager of the Cattle and Slave Market
(*amīn-i penṭh-i nakhās*)

* Headman of remaining markets (*chaudhurīs*)
(not given)

Superintendent of the Cattle and Slave Market (*dārogha*)

* Denotes local incumbents of offices

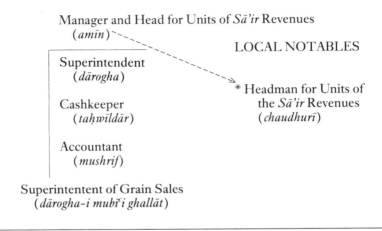

English Translation of the Document Forms

List of Contents of Official Appointment Orders (*asnād*) for Positions (filled by) Imperial Servants and for Claimants of Salary Totalling Sixty-Five Orders

Notes

1 This is a translation of the list provided by the compiler. The folio numbers have been added. The original manuscript was not paginated. Throughout the text, the compiler has given all headings in the impersonal possessive form. *Ṣūbadārī*, for example, could be translated as "of the governorship", but for the sake of simplicity, has been rendered using the personal noun, "governor" (or "superintendent" instead of "superintendency").

Details of Appointment Orders for Posts According to the Exalted Office

215b

Position of Governor (*Ṣūbadār*)

(The post) is conferred in accordance with the imperial rescript of most sublime authority (*farmān wālā shān*).

215b

Position of Deputy Governor (*Nā'ib Nāẓim*)

This warrant (*sanad*) for the deputy governorship emanates from the exalted office of the *khaliṣa sharīf*[1]. According to the exalted command, the position of deputy governor of ______ province (*ṣūba*), previously conferred upon ______ of the highest grandeur, is entrusted to ______ of dauntless courage and high dignity.

He must make an extraordinary effort to bring order and prosperity to that province; to protect and secure (its) cities; to chastise and punish malefactors and rebels; to eradicate and suppress those who incite sedition; to make the roads and highways safe and secure; to assist and aid the *faujdārs*, the *amīns* of the *maḥals* of the *khāliṣa sharīf* and *pāybāqī* and the agents (*gumāshtas*) of the *jāgīrdārs*; to prevent the imposition of taxes forbidden by the exalted court, and to abolish forbidden articles and intoxicating liquors. He must take absolute care to see that no one among the strong can prey upon the weak.

The responsible officers, revenue collectors and *faujdārs* must accept the aforementioned *khān* as deputy governor (*nā'ib nāẓim*) of that province. They must recognize the reach of his authority and power in matters pertaining to his office (as governor). And they must not exceed the bounds of proper, advisable and appropriate behavior with that aforementioned just *khān*.

Notes

1 Orders for the posting of provincial governors came from the *dīwān* of the central reserved lands and revenue units (the *khāliṣa sharīf*). He and the *dīwān-i tan*, or *dīwān* of salaries, were immediate subordinates of the chief *dīwān* for the empire at the central office. *See* Jadunath Sarkar, *Mughal Administration*, pp. 35–36.

215b

Position of *Dīwān* of the Province

In conformity with the exalted order the position of *dīwān* (chief fiscal officer) of ______ province is transferred from ______ and conferred

216a upon ______ from the beginning of ______ season, according to the details specified on the reverse (of this order).[1] He must fulfill the duties and customary obligations of that position with rectitude and propriety.[2] He must not permit the slightest matter to escape his vigilance and care in the *maḥals* of the central reserved lands of that province (the *k̲h̲āliṣa sharīf*); in comforting and keeping peace among the peasants; in promoting the increase of population; in nurturing a flourishing prosperity; and in expanding cultivation. And he must make certain that the revenue collectors (*ʿummāl*) do not demand from the peasants more than half of the *k̲h̲arāj* (which is measured and established by the illumined *sharīʿa* [law] and the path of the exalted *khalīfat* most pure) and thus that the peasants suffer no damage or loss. He must not permit the (most) powerful landed aristocrats (*zamīndārs*) to retain (excessive) profits on their estates. He must stay alert to repel grasping or embezzling collectors (*ʿummāl*), revenue agents (*karōṛīyān*) and treasurers (*fūṭadārān*). He must ensure that revenue collectors do not use terror or oppression to collect from the peasants the cess on tax collection (*taḥṣīldārī*), the tax on certificates (*paṭṭadārī*), or the travel costs of officials (*ṣādir wārīd*), that the benevolence-diffusing Throne has forgiven the peasants for their own welfare.

And if any of the revenue collectors defrauds or embezzles his fees from the village treasury, or collects forbidden levies, or oppresses (the taxpayers), he (the *dīwān*) must discover the essential truth of that person's behavior. He must do this in such a way that, any future (imperial) investigation will not contradict (his previous report). And (his actions) should not have any selfish motives, which are despicable in
216b (official) affairs. He must write (the report) to transmit this information to the sacred and exalted ruler, who alone will appoint another person in (that officer's) place. By no means, may he (the *dīwān*) have the boldness to transfer or dismiss (anyone) without an exalted order.

From every collector who may be dismissed, he (the *dīwān*) must demand restitution and the payment of any outstanding balances. After confronting him (the dismissed officer) in person, the *dīwān* must then send him to His Majesty's court where upon his arrival, the necessary computations (of arrears or embezzlements) will be carried out. Keeping to the path of circumspection, the *dīwān* must collect in every season the account papers of the several villages of every subdistrict (*pargana*), and translate them into Persian.[3] If this process reveals that the collectors have seized money through forbidden taxes or from the *dīwān's* allowances, he must demand restitution from them in face-to-face meetings. He should send the translated accounts to His Majesty so that a fit and appropriate punishment may be determined. He must keep the delinquent collectors in confinement as a warning to other embezzlers. In the event that no evidence of misappropriation by the collector (is) revealed, he should retain the collector in office.

According to established rules, he must send to the exalted record office, the *dīwān's* copies (or summaries), the rolls, and other papers, season by season and year by year. He must take a bond from the headmen and accountants that they will reveal the details of any embezzlement and (the collection of) exempted cesses by the collectors. If they lie and are negligent in reporting that (problem) he may petition that (these local officers) be dismissed and expelled from their ancestral holdings (*mauṭin*) and from their habitations.

He must proclaim the right of the collectors to realize, in the demarcated villages of every *maḥal*, an additional five rupees for every one hundred rupees of the current revenue demand set by the assessors in every harvest season, this additional sum to be applied against the total arrears and advance payments (*taqāwī*) owed by the peasants since the forty-second year in the reign of the deceased Emperor Aurangzeb.
217a In the earliest revenue collections of the current year, the *dīwān* must include the monies outstanding from agricultural loans (advances) for the previous year, together with the (outstanding) arrears from that year.

He must withhold from the allowances of the collection officers (*karoṛīyān*) (the deduction) of one rupee per hundred against possible (claims arising from a future) audit. He may allow the officers to receive the remainder (of the allowances) in conformity with their individual warrants. If from time to time the aforesaid allowance is not sufficient to pay the collectors' fees, he may disburse the requisite amount from the revenue proceeds of the current year.

The responsible officers of that place must accept the aforementioned person as *dīwān* bearing full authority. They must recognize that the duties and customary rights of that position belong to him. They must realize that his and no other's hand can exercise power in the affairs attached to that position and its responsibilities. They are to know that there are strict injunctions in this matter.

Notes

1 This word presents some difficulty in translation. The supporting documents such as the bond (*muchulkā*) were often entered on the reverse of a *sanad* of appointment and in this sense the term *ẓimn* could be read as (*ẓamn*) surety or security. However, *ẓimn* can also mean endorsement or enclosure, or even the cover or fold of a letter. Whether the former or the latter rendering is more accurate is uncertain given that the more common term for surety paid by *manṣabdārs* was *ẓāmin*. *See* M. Athar Ali, *Mughal Nobility*, p. 60, who stresses that "every candidate for a *manṣab* had to provide a surety (*ẓāmin*) and this rule was very rigorously enforced." Yet this rule applied to the initial acceptance of an officer into the imperial service, not necessarily for each post to which he was sent. Pending further explanation I have rendered *ẓimn* as "the details specified on the reverse" in the remaining orders.

2 Apart from this initial, essentially stereotyped, statement of his duties, we might expect that any imperial officer occupying a position as critically important as that of the chief fiscal officer of a province would regularly receive other, more specific, instructions and communications. Obviously, the

wazīr or head imperial *dīwān* and his two colleagues at the center were in continual correspondence and communication with the provincial *dīwāns*. The greater part of the surviving archival documents from the Inayat Jang Collection, for example, offer ample proof of that. In addition, however, the head *dīwān* and the Emperor regularly issued general directives to all the *dīwāns* of the Empire. In one of the first scholarly editions of such a document, Jadunath Sarkar identified an imperial *farmān* or edict of the Emperor Aurangzeb issued in the year A.D. 1668–69 (1079 A.H.) to Mohammad Hashim. He discovered this edict simply by studying the manuscript catalogue of the Berlin Royal Library. Sarkar published the text and a careful translation of this document in 1906. In the same essay, he also published the text and translation of a similar imperial edict sent to an unnamed revenue collector (*karoṛī*). Each document appears to be one copy of a general encyclical. The *farmān* addressed to the *dīwān* contains eighteen clauses. Each clause sets out specific procedures and policies for the *dīwān*. The fourth clause, for example, instructs the *dīwān* to investigate fallow or waste land (*uftāda*): If it is in the path of fixed roads or highways it should remain fallow; in all other cases the *dīwān* should find the owner and force him to have it cultivated. These clauses amplify the general instructions found in the appointment order translated above. None either contradicts or violates the formulas given in the present document. Cf. Jadunath Sarkar, "The Revenue Regulations of Aurangzib," *Journal of the Asiatic Society of Bengal* 2, N. S. (1906): 225–255. *See also* Sarkar, *Mughal Administration*, pp. 176–198, for the English translation of these two documents minus the text.

3 Village records kept by the village accountant were written in Hindi or in other regional languages. *See* Habib, *The Agrarian System*, p. 135. The records kept at the level of the *pargana* may also have been in the local languages for reference purposes, but were certainly translated into Persian when forwarded beyond this level.

217a

Position of *Faujdār* and *Amīn*[1]

Presently, according to the exalted order, the position of *faujdār* and *amīn* of ______ subdistrict, ______ district, ______ province, is transferred from ______ and conferred upon ______, from the beginning of ______ season, according to the details specified upon the reverse of this document.

He (the appointee) must fulfill completely the duties and customary obligations of that position with rectitude and propriety. He must not permit the slightest matter to escape his vigilance and care. He must exert every effort to maintain order, to punish malefactors and rebels, to destroy the strongholds of such groups, to protect and succour the imperial subjects (*zīr-dastān*) and the local revenue payers (*mālguzārān*), and to prevent smiths from manufacturing firearms. He must order his *thānadārs*, (military commanders of fortified posts) who are appointed to keep order, not to exact any of the forbidden taxes. If malefactors have become unruly and seditious in any particular village from among the
217b villages of those subdistricts, and the revenue collector has given a written statement concerning their punishment, he (the *faujdār*) must

first seize a number of them (the rebels). (He must) attempt to reform them so that they may repent of their stubborn and refractory ways, agree to pay their taxes, and submit to authority. Upon successful reform (of these persons) he must obtain a certificate of satisfaction from the revenue collector. However, if due to their inherent deceitful villainy they will not reform, he may attack that aforesaid village and punish the malefactors. Yet he must not harm the smaller cultivators (in this process). Any plunder that he may capture (from that village) such as livestock, etc., he must turn over to the revenue collector, from whom he must obtain a receipt. He may also confiscate for the state a penalty equal to the proper land revenue demand for the aforesaid village. He should not take captives save in the Land of War (*Dār al-ḥarb*).[2]

He must guard the royal roads so that travellers and wayfarers may move back and forth with composed and tranquil minds. Nowhere may he permit theft and highway robbery. If the property (or goods) of any person is stolen or plundered, he must recover (it) from the thieves and highwaymen, and return such property to its rightful owner. He must punish the band of miscreants. And if he cannot recover (the property), he himself must replace (the value of) the aforesaid goods.[3]

He should take special care that forbidden articles and intoxicating liquors are not used in those subdistricts.

He must promote zealously the welfare and tranquility of the peasantry and increase cultivation in every village. He must fully inform himself of the proceeds from every kind of crop. Every year, utilizing his knowledge and experience, he must establish the land revenue demand (*jama*^{c}). (He must do this) after inspecting every village in the cultivated area, and inquiring into the condition of the peasantry, in order that the smaller peasants may not suffer hardship, and in order that powerful persons may
218a not seize any surplus. (In setting the revenue demand) he must (apportion) half of the whole (anticipated proceeds of the harvest) to the peasant, and half, with no diminution, to the exalted state.

He (the *faujdār* and *amīn*) must firmly order the collector (*karoṛī*) to deliver all revenue to the treasurer once it has been collected. He must also direct the collector to liquidate the total arrears owed by the peasants since the forty-second year in the reign of the deceased Emperor Aurangzeb, by collecting five additional rupees per one hundred rupees of the current revenue demand set for every season. (He must order the collector) to recover the amount of any advances paid to the peasants in the previous year, along with any outstanding arrears of taxes from that same year, in the first returns of the current year. In case of negligence or delay, he (the *amīn*) will be investigated. (The *amīn*) must be vigilant against any rash collector who would dare to seize his perquisites from the village treasuries without authorization, or to exact taxes forbidden by the exalted court.[4]

He should recognize that, in conformity with established rules, he is personally responsible for the protection of the monies in the charge of the treasurer. He is (also responsible) for repaying the arrears of any amount (charged to him) from the land revenue or from stores. He must be alert to see that the treasurer does not spend a single *dām* without an authentic warrant from the *dīwān*. Having caused the aforesaid monies to be sent to the general treasury, he must ensure that the treasurer obtains a receipt for the total sum.

In accordance with accepted practice, he should deduct from the allowances of the *karoṛī* (the collector) one rupee (per hundred) to be held against any (claims arising from a future) audit. He must enter this in the revenue demand (*jamaᶜ*) so that henceforward this (escrow) allowance will be established (in anticipation of) the collector's audit. He (the *amīn*) under his own authority (certification) may take the balance (of the collector's salary) from the arrears and advances collected, and may pay the collector's fee. In the event that the aforesaid sum does not suffice to pay the collector, he may make up the full sum from the proceeds of the
218b current year's[5] revenue collections. Having prepared the revenue roll and other account papers for every harvest season, he must send them to His Resplendent Majesty.

The subdistrict headmen and accountants, the village headmen, peasants, and cultivators of that place must accept the aforementioned person as *faujdār* and *amīn* of those *maḥals*. They must heed the prudent words and good opinions of the aforementioned person who is indeed held accountable (literally, surety) for (responsible) management, for furthering the affairs and interests of the sublime state, for the welfare of the peasants and taxpayers and the security of the populace. They must recognize that the duties and customary rights of that position belong to him.

Note

1 For a translation of the appointment order for a *faujdār* alone, taken from a similar administrative manual, *see* Qeyam Uddin Ahmad, "The Functioning of Some of the Provincial and Local Officials of the Mughal Government," in the *Proceedings of the Indian History Congress* (1958): 353.

2 This is the Mughal expression of the long-standing Indian notion that those officers responsible for maintaining order must respond to any theft in the territory under their charge by either recovering the stolen goods or compensating the victims for their losses. Cf. Qureshi, *Administration of the Mughal Empire*, p. 206.

3 William Norris, the English ambassador sent to the Emperor Aurangzeb's court-camp in A.D. 1700–1702, gave an account of this principle in operation. When Norris arrived near the Emperor's camp and set up his own camp next to a small town, the superintendent (*dārogha*) and the town magistrate (*kotwāl*) paid him a visit and asked him to move his camp closer to the town so that they could provide him with a sufficient guard, as the Emperor had ordered. When Norris refused on the grounds his own armed guard could look after his security, both officers remonstrated with him "and declared that they would not be answerable for any loss he might sustain through robbery. They therefore asked him to give them a written document which would free them of any responsibility if he should be robbed." Harihar Das, *The Norris Embassy to Aurangzib, 1699–1702* (Calcutta, 1959, pp. 255–256).

4 "[P]erquisites from village treasuries" is an awkward translation of the term *malbā*. In *The Agrarian System* Habib interprets this as a narrow administrative usage of the Hindi *malbā*, meaning all expenditures for and by village officers on behalf of the entire community (pp. 126–127n, 243n). In this instance, the Mughal administration seems to have used the term to mean illegal extortions from a village by its own officers, which would have been entered into the village records as one type of *malbā* or expenditure. Cf. Wilson, *Glossary of Judicial and Revenue Terms*, p. 324 *Malbā*, Hindi "Village expenses [such as] feeding religious mendicants, payments to subordinate police and revenue officers, allowance for village watchmen, renumeration to individuals for losses incurred in supplying cattle and carts for public service . . . the total varied from 10 to 12 per cent on the public assessment." The present text spells *malba* without the long vowel.

5 *See* Habib, *The Agrarian System*, pp. 279–280, for a discussion of the mode of paying *karoṛīs'* allowances. Habib cites a passage from the administrative manual, *Nigār-nāma-i Munshī*, using terms similar to those in this text.

218b

Faujdār of a *Jāgīr*[1]

Presently, according to the exalted order, the position of *faujdār* for ______ assignment (*jāgīr*) (consisting of) ______ dāms allocated to salary in ______ *pargana*, ______ district, ______ province, has been transferred from ______ and placed in charge of ______, according to the details specified on the reverse. Having undertaken the duties and customary obligations of that position, he must act as follows:

He must exert every effort to maintain order, to punish malefactors and rebels, to destroy the strongholds of such groups, to protect and succour the imperial subjects and the local revenue payers, and to prevent smiths from manufacturing firearms. He must ensure that the body of men whom he deploys at the fortified posts (*thānajāt*) of the subdivisions (*maḥal*) of his assigned territory are used strictly to collect revenue and maintain order. He is ordered not to collect any of the forbidden taxes or cesses. He must not permit anyone to use forbidden articles or intoxicating liquors.

If malefactors have become unruly and seditious in any particular village of those *maḥals*, he must first seize a number (of the rebels). (He must) attempt to reform them so that they repent of their stubborn and
219a refractory ways, agree to pay their taxes, and submit to authority. However, if due to their inherent deceitful villainy, they will not reform, he may attack that village and punish the malefactors. He must not harm nor take captive any imperial subjects save in the Land of War.

He must guard the royal roads in such a manner that travellers and wayfarers may move back and forth with composed and tranquil minds. In no place may he permit theft and highway robbery. If the property of any person is stolen or plundered, he must recover it from the thieves and highwaymen and return the goods to their rightful owner. He must punish that band of miscreants. If he cannot recover the stolen property he himself must replace (the value of) the aforesaid goods.

The district and *pargana* headmen, district and *pargana* accountants, peasants, village headmen, and cultivators (*muzāriʿān*) of that place must strictly accept the aforementioned person as *faujdār* of the *maḥals* (subdivision or fiscal divisions) of that aforementioned *jāgīr*. They must also recognize that the duties and customary rights of that position (assignment) belong to him. They are to know that there are strict injunctions in this matter.

Notes

1 Strictly speaking, under the Mughal system of administration, the officer or nobleman holding a salary assignment or *jāgīr* for the pay of himself and his followers, possessed a fiscal claim only for the revenue from a specified fiscal entity – usually a bounded territory producing a fixed amount of land tax on agrarian production. The assignment holder thus did not possess either the obligation or the right to maintain order. The officer holding a larger *jāgīr* assignment might, however, request an appointment as a *faujdār* of his *jāgīr*, which authorized him to employ troops and to administer fully the area assigned to him. He could then protect his revenues by anticipating and moving against political unrest or lax collection by the imperial and local officials. He could also use his privately employed officers, agents and soldiers as tax collectors. *See* Richards, *Mughal Administration in Golconda*, pp. 196–199, for a discussion of this point and examples from Aurangzeb's reign. For a detailed view of the *jāgīr* system, *see* Ḥabib, *The Agrarian System*, pp. 257–197, and M. Athar Ali, *Mughal Nobility*, pp. 74–94, especially page 87 for *faujdārī* rights over salary assignment lands.

219a

The Position of Revenue Collector (*Karoṛī*)

At this time, according to the exalted order, the position of revenue collector for ______ subdistrict, ______ district and province, is transferred from ______ and conferred upon ______, from the beginning of ______ (date) in conformity with the details specified on the reverse of this document. He (the appointee) must fulfill the duties and customary obligations of that position with rectitude and propriety.

He must exert every effort to increase the area's population, wealth, and prosperity, to promote agriculture, and to resettle the peasants, He must collect to the last *dām* the revenues and *dīwān's* fees levied by the revenue assessor (the *amīn*) from those fiscal units (*maḥals*). He must deliver those proceeds to the treasurer's charge. He may not withhold a single *dām*. He should shun any exaction of his personal expenses from village funds (*malba*) or the exaction of forbidden levies. He should set
219b aside one percent from his own allowances against any future claims arising from an audit. He should collect the remainder (of his fees) from the money (outstanding) for arrears and advances, after (obtaining) the written approval of the *amīn*. Acting in cooperation with the *amīn*, he must collect in every harvest season an additional sum of five rupees per hundred rupees of the current revenue demand fixed by the assessor for

every village. (This will recover) the arrears and advances owed by the peasants from past revenue years, dating from the forty-second year in the reign of the deceased Emperor Aurangzeb. In the earliest revenue returns of the current year, he must obtain the monies loaned to the peasants for the previous (past) year as agricultural advances by the exalted state. He will be responsible for restitution in the event of carelessness or delay.

He must bring to the treasury all money paid by the peasants and he must be sure they are given a receipt (*chiṭṭhī*) bearing both his seal and the signature of the treasurer. At the time of payment in full (by the peasants), he should compute the total revenue received (from them) as the total of those same receipts. Apart from the money rightfully due, he may take nothing in the form of complimentary gifts,[1] payments for his own expenses or fees (*taḥṣīldārī*), or any other charges from local funds (*malba*). According to regulations and recognized practice, he must send to the exalted office the abstracts, income and expense statements, and other account papers.

The district and subdistrict headmen and accountants, village headmen, peasants and cultivators (*muzāriᶜān*) of those *maḥals* shall accept the aforementioned person as collector of that place. They must recognize that the duties and customary rights of that position belong to him.

Notes

1 The term from Hindi is *bheṅṭ*. Cf. Wilson, *Glossary*, p. 80: "the presentation of a gift made to a superior on occasion of being presented or introduced to him . . . . A present made by the cultivator to the collector or farmer on settling his assessment."

219b

Position of Treasurer (*Fūṭadār*)

At this time, the position of treasurer (*fūṭadār*) of ______ subdistrict, of ______ district and province, is transferred from ______ and conferred upon ______ at the beginning of ______ (date) to ______ (date), in accordance with the details specified (*ẓimn*).

He (the appointee) must fulfill the duties and customary obligations of
220a that position with rectitude and propriety. He must not permit the slightest matter to escape his vigilance and care.

He must deposit the tax revenues collected from his area carefully in his cash box (or vault). He must lock the door of that vault and secure it with his seal and that of the *amīn*. Only acting jointly (with the *amīn*), should he open and close (that door). He must not expend a single *dām* without an authentic warrant from the *dīwān*. Upon consultation with the *amīn* (and upon his advice), he must send all the cash in his charge to the general treasury of the province (*khizāna'-i ᶜāmira*) and obtain a receipt.

The officers (responsible for various duties) of that area must accept the aforementioned person as treasurer of those *maḥals*. They must also recognize that the duties and customary rights of that position belong to him. Whatever tax proceeds are realized they must turn over personally to his charge. They must hold nothing whatsoever back.

They are to know that there are strict injunctions in this matter.

220a **Position of Pargana Headman (*Chaudhurī*) and Accountant (*Qānūngo*)**[1]

The responsible officers and those persons in charge of affairs at present and in the future are hereby informed: at this time, according to the exalted order, the position of headman or accountant of ______ subdistrict (*pargana*) is transferred from ______, and established and conferred (on ______ contingent) upon payment of ______ (amount) in tribute (*peshkash*) to the elevated state, in accordance with the details specified on the reverse of this document.[2] He (the recipient) must fulfill the duties and customary obligations of that position. He must work strenuously to enhance the popularity and prosperity of the exalted state, to resettle the peasants and promote their welfare, and to enlarge the area of cultivation.
220b He must not permit the slightest matter to escape his vigilance and care.

In conformity with fixed regulations and custom, year by year, he (the nominee) must despatch to the exalted office the record of revenue and area taxed for the past decade (*muwāẓana*), the record of cash revenue rates for each crop (*dastūr al-ʿamal*), and other papers from the accounts for the collections and assessment of the current year, etc., for the perusal of the provincial *dīwān*.[3]

He must not create violent strife and discord. He should gratify the peasants, nobles, and other inhabitants of that place by his upright conduct. He must avoid embezzlement and oppression. Save for the established customary fees, he may take no avaricious demand whatsoever of anyone.

The subdistricts headmen and accountants, the village headmen, and the peasants must accept the aforementioned person as accountant of that place. They must heed his prudent speech and righteous conduct provided that he attends to the prosperity of the exalted state and the tranquility of the peasants and the cultivators in conformity with every provision of the details specified on the reverse of this document. They are to know that there are strict injunctions in this matter.

Notes

1 Although this model letter is intended to appoint a joint headman and accountant, the more usual practice seems to have been to make separate appointments for each office. Cf. Richards, *Mughal Administration in Golconda*, pp. 138–147.

2 Generally, *peshkash* or tribute was any sort of presentation, usually money, made by subordinate officials or by tributary rulers, local chiefs or local notables to the Emperor or to higher officers of the empire. In this context *peshkash* refers to the practice of demanding that new subdistrict headmen and accountants pay a bond equivalent to the income from their new offices over

six and one-half years, in order to confirm their appointments. This type of demand, and the term *peshkash*, were not conditions of appointment for regular imperial officers of officials, but characterized the appointment of a local notable to a local office. Cf. Richards, *Mughal Adminstration in Golconda*, pp. 187–88, and Habib, *The Agrarian System*, pp. 184–185.

3 The second paragraph of the letter in translation incorporates two complex technical terms: *muwāzana* and *dastūr al-^{c}amal.* The former is an abbreviation of the term *muwāzana-i dah sāla*, which Habib translates in *The Agrarian System*, p. 219, as "record of the revenue and area of the last ten years." In this context the term refers to the land revenue proceeds and measured cultivated area for the past ten revenue years in the *pargana* in question. The *dīwān* maintained this record, (updated annually by dropping the earliest revenue year and adding the current year's figures) to check the valuation or assessment (*jama^{c}dāmī*) setting the revenue demand for the *pargana* and, if necessary, to adjust in this. The *dastūr al-^{c}amal* records document the rate in cash demanded for each crop per unit of area for either the spring or fall harvest. These rates applied to groupings of subdistricts with similar soil, climate and other conditions of production. Taken together these two sets of records were vital for the regulation Mughal system of cash assessment on measured cultivated areas known as the *ẓabt* system. *See* Habib, *The Agrarian System*, pp. 190–212, for a discussion of the origin and operation of this system.

220b

The Position of *Zamīndār*[1]

The responsible officers and those persons in charge of affairs, the headmen (*chaudhurīyān*), accountants, village headmen of ______ sub-district, ______ district and province are hereby informed: at this time, according to the exalted order, the position of *zamīndār* of the aforesaid *maḥals* is transferred from ______ and conferred upon ______ upon payment of the sum of ______ (amount) in tribute (*peshkash*) to the exalted state in accordance with the details specified on the reverse of this document. He (the recipient) must fulfill the duties and customary obligations of that position, (in such a way that) he may gratify all of the peasants and aristocrats (*barāyā*) by his conduct.

He must devote great effort to expelling, punishing and disciplining any
221a malefactors and (other) obstinately rebellious persons. He must clear every trace of thieves and highwaymen from that territory. He must promote the welfare and tranquility of the peasantry; increase cultivation and settlement; and inspire loyalty and goodwill (towards the state). He must so act that the seditions will have absolutely no possibility of interfering in that *maḥal.* He should guard the royal roads in such a manner that travellers and wayfarers may move back and forth with composed and tranquil minds and that no theft or highway robbery may take place. If the property of any person is stolen or plundered, he must search out the thieves and highwaymen, return the goods to their rightful owner and punish that band of miscreants. If he cannot recover the property, he must reimburse the owner for the (value of the) stolen goods.

He must see that no one within the boundaries belonging to his territory (*zamīndārī*) uses forbidden articles and intoxicating liquors.

The inhabitants of the aforesaid *maḥals* must accept the aforementioned person as *zamīndār* and recognize the duties and customary rights of that position as belonging to him.

Notes

1 The duties specified here for a locally dominant warrior-aristocrat (largely non-Muslims from the Hindu dominant castes) are entirely martial and magisterial rather than fiscal. The acknowledged obligation of the *zamīndār* to pay the land revenue for all lands under his jurisdiction does not appear in this letter of appointment. Nor do we find any mention of the 10 percent allowance usually granted for that service. Certainly, these arrangements may have been set out in the administrative specifications recorded on the reverse of this letter when it was actually composed, but the central obligation of the *zamīndār* in the standard text of this document is to maintain order and peace as a loyal servant of the imperial administration. *See* Habib, *The Agrarian System*, pp. 136–182, especially, pp. 146, 151, and 170. Habib suggests that *zamīndārs* often served as intermediaries for the collection of the land tax. Nevertheless, the *zamīndār's* fiscal role is virtually ignored in the normative revenue literature, whether because it was taken for granted or because it was distasteful to the Mughal ideal of a direct relationship between imperial officer and peasant.

221a **Position of Auditor of Accounts (*Barāmad-nawīs*)**

The responsible officers of ______ district and province are hereby informed that, according to the exalted order, the position of auditor of the accounts of the tax collectors dismissed from that place is transferred from ______ and placed in the charge of ______ according to the details specified on the reverse (of this order). He must fulfill the duties and obligations of that position with rectitude and propriety. He must not
221b permit the slightest matter to escape his vigilance and care. He must audit the dismissed collectors by checking (their work) against the original draft papers (village and *pargana* accounts).[1] These should be free of any suspicion of forgery. (He must work to see that) the accounts conceal or hide nothing and that none of the collectors is either persecuted or favored.

Having verified them (the collectors' amounts) with the cooperation of superintendent of the provincial treasury,[2] in the presence of the collectors' agents, he must prepare the rolls (summary accounts) according to fixed regulations. He must send these (the completed accounts), bearing his and the superintendent's certification and the signatures of the *chaudhurīs* and *qānūngos*, to the exalted office so that the required restitution and deduction (of fines or arrears from the officials' salaries) may be completed.

They (the responsible officers) must accept the aforementioned person as auditor for those fiscal units (*maḥals*). They must recognize that the duties and customary rights of that position belong to him. They must also not delay (him) in summoning and deploying the *chaudhurīs*, *qānūngos*, headmen (*muqaddamān*) and officers and other agents, or the accounts and papers, which he may (need) for his investigation of these matters. (Finally) they must cooperate fully with the aforementioned officer in all his work.

Notes

1 Cf. Habib, *The Agrarian System*, p. 280: "The accounts of the actual collections of the *ʿamils* and their agents were audited in many cases by the help of the village *patwaris'* [*i.e.* village accountants'] papers . . . this method of audit, known as *barāmad*, [was] a part of the routine of administration." Habib refers to actual cases of such audits as well as to the normative manuals. Qureshi relies upon this model letter of appointment for his citation, in *Administration of the Mughul Empire*, pp. 158–59.

2 The text simply states: "with the superintendent (*dārogha*)," which probably refers to the *dārogha* of the provincial treasury and overseer of provincial reports, whose duties are set out (and translated here) in folio 237b.

221b **Order (*Parwāna*), in a Fair Copy, for the *Faujdārs* and *Amīns***

Let all those (nobles) who are the refuge of dignity and the fount of courage and tenacity impress this upon their memory: at this time, according to the exalted order, the position of *amīn* and *faujdār* of ______ subdivision, ______ district and province from the beginning of ______ to ______ is conferred upon and entrusted to that refuge of dignity.

(The appointee), having acknowledged his gratitude for this muni-
222a ficence,[2] must exert every effort to: punish malefactors and rebels; protect and succour the lowly subjects and the taxpayers; secure the land revenue due to the sublime state (the Emperor); expand cultivation; and increase population.

When he has made the collection, in accordance with the revenue assessment, he must send (that money) to the Resplendent Emperor by means of reliable drafts (*huṇḍwīyāt*) drawn on reliable money changers (*ṣarrāfān*).

Subsequently, when the agent (*wakīl*), of that refuge of dignity (the appointee) has received a warrant (*sanad-i ẓimnī*) confirming this appointment, he will send it (back).[1]

Notes

1 This form refers to an officer stationed at the Emperor's court as the private agent (*wakīl*) of the Mughal commander in question. Some of the activities of these figures who are still rather shadowy in the historical record could explain much about the actual operation of the imperial system. Such officers seem to have performed the work of fiscal agent, lobbyist, legal counsel or representative, and attendant at court – not to mention a number of other less savory functions, such as spying.

2 The 'gratitude' referred to here could be either a substantial monetary offering to the emperor (*peshkash*), or merely the ceremonial offering of a few coins (*naẕr*) on the occasion of an official appointment. *See* M. Athar Ali, *Mughal Nobility*, pp. 143–144, for a discussion of such presents.

222a

Position of Superintendent of the Subdistrict Treasury

This order is issued to the responsible officers of the treasury of ______ *pargana*, ______ district and province: at this time, according to the exalted order, the superintendency of the aforementioned treasury is transferred from ______ and conferred upon ______. He must fulfill the duties and customary obligations of that position with rectitude and propriety. He must not permit the slightest matter to escape his vigilance and care.

He must (ensure) the complete security of the treasury. He must deposit all collected funds in the safety of the treasury. He must lock the door of that vault and secure it with his seal and that of the treasurer. Only in his presence may it be opened or closed. He must send that cash, scrupulously, in accordance with established rules and fixed regulations, to the general treasury (of the province) accompanied by the *faujdār's* escort. He must be sure to provide a receipt for the treasurer (of the *pargana*).

He must not expend a single *dām* without an authentic warrant from the *dīwān*. He must curtail the grasp of embezzlement or fraud from any direction.

They (the responsible officers) must accept the aforementioned person as superintendent of the aforesaid treasury. They must recognize that the duties and customary rights of this position belong to him.

222a

Position of Cash Keeper (*Taḥwīldār*) of the *Maḥals* of *Sā'ir*[1]

222b This order is issued to the responsible officers of ______ *maḥals* of *sā'ir* of ______ province: at this time the position of cash keeper of the aforementioned fiscal units is transferred from ______ and placed in the charge of ______. In fulfilling the duties and obligations of that position with rectitude and propriety, he must not permit the slightest matter to escape his vigilance and care.

He must keep the monies in his charge with the utmost prudence in the cash chest (*koṭhī*), under his own seal and that of the superintendent (of the *sā'ir*). He must not expend a single *dām* without an authentic warrant from the *dīwān* (of the province). With the approval of the collector (*amīn* of *sā'ir*), he must send all of the cash in his charge to the general treasury of the province and obtain a receipt.

They (the officers mentioned) must accept the aforesaid person as cash keeper of those *maḥals*. They must recognize that the duties and customary rights of that position belong to him. Whatsoever they may receive from the tax collections of that place, they are to give into his charge, holding nothing back.

Notes

1 For a discussion of the multifarious imposts collected under the *sā'ir* administration of the Mughals, *see* Richards, *Mughal Administration in Golconda*, pp. 185–191, *Sā'ir* collections, divided into fiscal units or *maḥals* for each revenue-producing category, included road customs, house taxes, octroi, and market taxes. Each major commodity market in a larger city was a separate *maḥal* for collecting *sā'ir* revenue. A local merchant-headman or *chaudhurī* divided responsibility for regulation of these market units with a petty official, the *muqīm*. Cf. Richards, *Mughal Administration in Golconda*, pp. 187–188, for examples of this structure from Mughal official records for Hyderabad city in the late seventeenth century.

222b Position of Accountant (*Mushrif*) of the *Maḥals* of *Sā'ir*

This order is issued to the responsible officers of the revenue of ______ *maḥals* of *sā'ir* belonging to ______ province: at this time the position of accountant of that place is transferred from ______ and placed in the charge of ______. He must fulfill the duties and obligations of that position with rectitude and propriety. He must not permit the slightest matter to escape his vigilance and care.

Having prepared the papers (accounts) in conformity with fixed regulations and established rules, he must send (them) to the exalted office (of the province).

They (the officers mentioned) must accept him as accountant of that place. They must recognize that the duties and customary rights of that position belong to him.

223a Position of Secretary (*Peshkār*) to the *Amīn* and *Faujdār*

This order goes out to the most select contemporaries and peers: at this time, the position of secretary to the *faujdār* and *amīn* of ______ *maḥals*, is transferred from ______ and placed in the charge of ______. In fulfilling with rectitude and propriety the duties and obligations of that (position), he (the new appointee) must not permit the slightest matter to escape his vigilance and care.

In all the affairs of that place he must work frugally and keep himself carefully informed to prevent the loss or omission of a single *dām*. He must prepare detailed and corrected account papers in accordance with fixed regulations, and in conformity with firmly established rules, in order to send (these accounts) to the exalted office. They (the selected officers) are to know there are strict injunctions in this matter.

223a

Position of the Superintendent and Fiscal Officer (*Amīn*) of the Mint

This order is issued to the responsible officers, clerks and workmen of the mint located in ______ province: at this time, in accordance with the exalted order, the position of superintendent of the aforementioned *maḥals* is transferred from ______, and placed in the charge of ______. In fulfilling the duties and obligations of the position with rectitude and propriety he (the latter) must not permit the slightest matter to escape his vigilance and care. He must work assiduously to maintain the proceeds (revenues) of those *maḥals* (the mint) according to fixed regulations and firmly established rules, and to prevent even the slightest negligence or loss. The *ashrafī*, rupees (coins) etc. must be struck from the illustrious die with perfect calligraphy, weight and assay.

Recognizing his responsibility to protect and guard the money under
223b the treasurer's charge, he must not permit the expenditure of a
single *dām* without an authentic warrant from the *dīwān*.

They (the officers mentioned) must accept the aforementioned person as fiscal officer (*amīn*) of those *maḥals*, and must recognize that the duties and customary rights of that position belong to him. They are to know that there are strict injunctions in this matter.

223b

Position of Master Assayer (*Ṣāḥib-ʿIyār*) of the Mint

This order is issued to the responsible officers, clerks and workmen of the mint located in ______ province: at this time the position of master assayer of the aforementioned *maḥals* is transferred from ______ and placed in the charge of ______.

He must fulfill the duties and obligations of that position with rectitude and propriety. He must not permit the slightest matter to escape his vigilance and care. He must cause the *ashrafī* (gold coins) and rupees (silver coins) etc. to reach the perfect assay, according to the regulations fixed for the current coin.[1]

They (the officers mentioned) must accept the aforementioned person as master assayer of that place. They must recognize that the duties and customary rights of that position belong to him.

Notes

1 The *sikka mubārak* was a term referring to coins minted during the current regnal year by any of the Mughal provincial mints. So-called 'sikka' coins passed at their face value with the money changers or at the state treasuries. Older coins bearing earlier dates circulated at a small discount, which probably allowed for wear in use. Such wear particularly affected coins with a high content of precious metals, including almost all Mughal coins. The best descriptive accounts of the Mughal monetary system and coinage remain that of Irfan Habib, "Currency System of the Mughal Empire, 1556–1707," in

Medieval India Quarterly 4, (1961): 1–21 and "The Monetary System and Prices" in Tapan Raychaudhuri and Irfan Habib eds. *The Cambridge Economic History of India* Volume I: c1200–c1750, Cambridge, 1982.

223b **Position of Headman (*Chaudhurī*) of the *Maḥals* of *Sā'ir***

This order is issued to the responsible officers, clerks and agents of the *maḥals* of *sā'ir* of ______ subdistrict, ______ province: at this time, the position of headman of the aforementioned *maḥals*, upon presentation of the sum of ______ (amount) rupees to the exalted state (ruler), is transferred from ______ and conferred upon ______.

In fulfilling with rectitude and propriety the duties and customary obligations of that position, he (the latter) must not permit the slightest matter to escape his vigilance and care. His upright conduct must satisfy the merchants and he must shun and repel all attempted cheating and embezzlement. He must work diligently to inspire goodwill (or support) among the population and to collect the revenues of the exalted state.
224a They (the officers mentioned) must accept the aforementioned person in the aforesaid position. They must recognize that the duties and customary rights of that position belong to him.

They are to know that there are strict injunctions in this matter.

224a **Position of Magistrate (*Kotwāl*) of the Imperial Camp (*Rikāb*), the "Stirrup", or of the City (*Balda*)**

This order is issued to the responsible officers, clerks and staff of the magistrate's office[1] of the Stirrup of Felicity (the Emperor's camp) or of ______ city in ______ province: at this time, in accordance with the exalted order, the position of magistrate of the aforementioned city is transferred from ______ and conferred upon ______.

He must fulfill the duties and customary obligations of that position with rectitude and propriety. He must not permit the slightest matter to escape his vigilance and care. Informing himself fully of the condition of the area's inhabitants, he must work energetically to impose order, protect the city, and to maintain the nightly watch and ward. He must prevent all theft. He must capture any thieves, recover the stolen property and return these goods to their rightful owner, and punish the thieves. If he cannot recover such goods, he must answer for the value of that (property) himself. He must diligently safeguard the population from assault or injury by ruffians. He must ensure that the inhabitants do not use intoxicating liquors and forbidden articles.[2] He (the magistrate) should implement the signed verdict of the judge (*qāẓī*) regarding the retention or release of persons imprisoned for crimes and (are) at the judge's disposition.

He should conduct himself properly with the inhabitants of that city,

224b and the clerks and staff of the magistrate's office. They (the officers and inhabitants) must accept the aforementioned person as magistrate of that place. They must recognize that the duties and customary rights of that position belong to him.

They are to know that there are strict injunctions in this matter.

Notes

1 Both the terms *kotwāl* and *chabūtara* (for establishment) are Hindi or Prakrit terms for an office which long antedates the Muslim conquest in South Asia. A number of officials in the Emperor's entourage were engaged solely to administer the moving city of the massive imperial camp. They accompanied the person of the Emperor whether he was on tour in camp ("the Stirrup of Felicity") or settled in a city. When the imperial household and the central administration settled in a city for a time, these officials often took over the urban offices as well – thus *kotwāl* of the Stirrup and the city. I am grateful to Stephen Blake for this observation.

2 The purely Islamic office which comes closest in its secular functions to some of the duties of the Indian *kotwāl*, is that of the *muḥtasib*, often translated as "censor", who regulated markets and tried to control the usage of wine and intoxicating drugs and other forbidden acts. Aurangzeb reinstated the office of *muḥtasib*, along with other sweeping policy changes, to make Mughal administration follow the *Sharīʿa* or Islamic law as closely as possible. In 1072 A.H./A.D. 1660 the Emperor issued a general order prohibiting the use of wine, *bhāṅg* (a beverage made from hemp), and other intoxicants. The newly appointed *muḥtasibs* and other executive officers in the empire were to enforce this edict. For a copy of the edict, *see* Ali Muhammad Khan, *Mir'āt-i Aḥmadī*, translated by M. F. Lokhandwala, number 146 in Gaekwad's Oriental Series (Baroda/[India], 1965), pp. 222–223. According to Muhammad Bakhtawar Khan, writing in the *Mir'āt al-ʿĀlam*, Aurangzeb issued this edict at the time of his second coronation. *See* Sajida S. Alvi, ed., *Mir'āt al-ʿĀlam*, vol. 1 (Lahore, 1979) published by the Research Society of Pakistan.

224b Position of Appraiser and Headman[1]

At this time the position of appraiser of ______ *maḥals* is transferred from ______ and conferred upon ______, so that he may fulfill the duties and customary obligations of that position with rectitude and propriety.

He must assess accurately the value of the goods that the merchants of those *maḥals* bring in so that no future investigation will reveal any discrepancy. Thereby the officers of that place according to the valuation may collect the (proper) revenues from that (merchandise) for the exalted state. Apart from the established rate, he must not take anything from the merchants. Having satisfied the merchants by his upright conduct, he must not embezzle or falsify even the slightest amount. In buying and selling he must work assiduously to prevent any shortfall in the revenues of the exalted state.

They (the officers mentioned) must accept him as the appraiser of that place. They must recognize that the duties and customary rights of that position belong to him.

They are to know that there are strict injunctions in this matter.

Notes

1 The terms employed here are *muqīm* (appraiser) and *mihtar* (headman). The latter term seems to refer to the head of a specific lower-ranking occupational group. Cf. Wilson, *Glossary*, p. 338: "Mehtar . . . the head of a caste or business, trade or art, who used to exercise considerable authority over the others." The valuation or appraisal referred to apparently fixed the empire-wide tax on goods, collected at the time of purchase in urban markets. Cf. Ali Muhammad Khan provides a copy of a royal order discussing this form of customs collection in Aurangzeb's reign, p. 284 in *Mirāt-i Aḥmadī*, translated by M. F. Lokhandwala and published by the Oriental Institute (Baroda, 1965).

224b Position of Superintendent of Canals[1]

This order is issued to the responsible officers, workmen, and laborers of the canal located in ______ place: in accordance with the exalted order, the position of superintendent of the aforementioned canal is transferred from ______ and conferred upon ______.

He, (the latter) must fulfill the duties and customary obligations of that position with rectitude and propriety. As established by custom, he must properly repair the canal at the time of sowing, with the assistance of the
225a peasants of the villages who use the water of that canal to irrigate their land. Thus he must ensure an abundant flow of water. He must divide and allocate (the water) in equal shares according to the cultivated area of each of the attached villages so that the populousness and produce of those *maḥals* will increase greatly, resulting in the prosperity of the state and the affluence of the peasants.

They (the officers mentioned) must accept the aforementioned person as superintendent of that place and recognize that the duties and customary rights of that position belong to him.

Notes

1 *See* Habib, *The Agrarian System*, pp. 31–36, for a description of the Mughal irrigation canal system in the north Indian plain, and for the functions of the canal superintendent.

225a Position of Superintendent of the Post (*Ḍākchaukī*)

This order is issued to ______: at this time by the order of Him Who Commands the World, the Resplendent (Emperor), the position of superintendent of the post of ______ province is transferred from ______ and conferred upon that refuge of dignity ______ (the nominee). He must fulfill the duties and customary obligations of that position. He must perform energetically and carefully (his duties) in the required manner. Thus he may ensure the arrival of the post-containers etc. for royal orders without any delay or hindrance.

He must convey, with strict care, the always felicitous imperial edicts and the divine orders issued to the officers of that place. He must despatch to His Resplendent Majesty petitions and news of events and occurrences in conformity with regulation and custom. He must take a bond from the messengers that they will allow nothing extraneous to accompany the containers for written (official) orders. He must ensure that they do not seize or confiscate cesses forbidden by the exalted court, or in any way interfere with travellers and wayfarers.

225b He must report suits in the court of justice, and provide detailed abstracts of the decisions, whether settlements or nonsettlements. He must reveal the particulars, including the condition and number of prisoners held in the fortresses and in the courts (*kachahrī*), and the reasons for their imprisonment.

He must describe (in his reports) the state of affairs of that place succinctly and truthfully, without any deletion or addition.

He should send these (reports) to the Emperor without delay or negligence. He must avoid both excessive partisanship and enmity (in his reporting). What more than this need be decreed?

225b

Position of Superintendent, and Using the Same Content, Collector for the *Maḥals* of Saffron

This order is issued to the responsible officers, workmen, and laborers of the *maḥals* of saffron of ______ subdistrict located in the province of Kashmir: at this time, the position of superintendent of the aforementioned fiscal units is transferred from ______ and conferred upon ______. In fulfilling the duties and customary obligations of that position with rectitude and propriety, he (the latter) must not permit the slightest matter to escape his vigilance and care. He must be assiduous and vigilant in his work during the season of flowering, picking (of the blossoms) and drying; in setting a price determined by the scarcity or abundance of saffron; increasing the profit for the state; and expanding the trade and sales to the customers.[1]

He must ensure that no one dares to cheat the buyers or adulterate (the saffron), and that the buyers themselves pay the full price of the saffron, leaving absolutely no arrears outstanding.

They (the officers mentioned) must accept him as the superintendent (bearing) absolute (powers). They must recognize that the duties and customary rights of that position belong to him. They are to know that
226a there are strict injunctions in this matter.

Notes

1 Saffron, produced only in Kashmir throughout the Mughal period, was a highly profitable state-controlled export. Cf. Habib, *The Agrarian System*, pp. 73, 75.

226a **Position of Superintendent, and Using the Same Content, the Collector of the Subdistrict Cattle and Slave Market (*Peṅṭh-i Nakhās*)**

This order is issued to the responsible officers, workmen, and staff of the cattle and slave market of ______ city, ______ province: at this time, the position of superintendent of that place is transferred from ______ and conferred upon ______. In fulfilling the duties and customary obligations of that position with rectitude and propriety, he (the latter) must not permit the slightest matter to escape his vigilance and care.

He must take charge of the collections in conformity with established custom and fixed regulations. He must keep himself well informed, to prevent any loss or negligence in all situations or transactions, and to repel any attempted embezzlement or fraud. The Hindu traders must not be able to intermingle their goods with (the goods traded by those) of the Muslim faith. He must take a bond to that effect from the brokers of that place. He must protect and guard the money (held) in the custody of the cashkeeper, so that the cashkeeper is not able to spend a single *dām* without an authentic warrant from the *dīwān*. All the monies in his (the cashkeeper's) charge must be sent to the provincial treasury and a receipt given to the cashkeeper.

They (the officers mentioned) must accept the aforementioned as superintendent of those *maḥals*. They must recognize that the duties and customary rights of that position belong to him.

226a **Position of Land Measurer (or Cadastral Surveyor)[1]**

This order is issued to the responsible officers of the *maḥals* or the royal lands[2]: at this time, the position of land measurer of those *maḥals* is transferred from ______ and conferred upon ______.

In fulfilling the duties and customary obligations of that position with rectitude and propriety, he (the latter) must not permit the slightest matter to escape his vigilance and care. He must send the account papers to the exalted office in conformity with established rules and fixed regulations.

They (the officers mentioned) must accept the aforesaid person as land measurer of those *maḥals*. They must recognize that the duties and customary rights of that position belong to him. They are to know that there are strict injunctions in this matter.

Notes

1 Wilson's *Glossary*, p. 389, translates *paimāna-kash* as a "weighman" or measurer, and associates the term with a number of similar terms referring to land surveying.

2 In *The Agrarian System*, p. 270, Habib describes the *khāliṣa sharīf* "as a group of assignments [*jāgīrs*] held directly by the imperial administration." In other

words, the imperial administration did not necessarily reserve for itself a fixed and bounded territory at the heart of the empire, but instead shifted the crown's possessions among the "most fertile and convenient lands."

226b **Bond (*Muchulkā*) for the Position of *Amīn* and *Faujdār***

I am the slave of the court, the Asylum of Mankind. As the *faujdārī* of ______ subdistrict belonging to ______ province has been assigned to the charge of this slave of the court and transferred from ______ by the seat of the *khilāfat* and world-conquering power, I am therefore submitting in writing (that):

I will fulfill the duties and customary obligations of that position with complete rectitude and propriety. I will not permit the slightest matter to escape my vigilance and care.

I will exert every effort to maintain order, to punish malefactors and rebels, to destroy the strongholds of those groups, to protect and succour the subjects and to prevent smiths from manufacturing firearms.

I will order that body (of officers) whom I appoint to the military posts (*thānajāt*) of the *maḥals* of the *faujdārī* (the area under his jurisdiction) not to seize anything in the form of forbidden taxes. No one from that place may use forbidden articles and intoxicating drugs.

If the headmen (*muqaddamān*) from any village (among) the villages (of my jurisdiction) have become unruly and seditious, I shall first seize a number and attempt to reform them by advice and persuasion. They must repent of their stubborn and evil ways, agree to pay the revenue demands, and submit to authority. However, if due to their inherent deceitful villainy they do not reform, I shall attack the aforesaid village and punish the malefactors.

I shall guard the royal roads in such a manner that travellers and wayfarers may move back and forth with composed and tranquil minds. Nowhere will I permit theft or highway robbery. If the property of any person is stolen or plundered I shall return the goods to the owner, and
227a punish that band (of thieves). If I cannot recover (the property), I shall personally reimburse the (rightful) owner for his losses.

I shall not expropriate the tax revenues (*māl*) of the *khāliṣa sharīf* or the *sā'ir*.

I have given these few words in the form of a bond in writing so that thereafter an order (*sanad*) may be issued.[1]

Note

1 As the last sentence in the text suggests, every recipient of an order of appointment, in this case a *sanad*, was required to sign a standard surety form called a bond (*muchulkā*), which put the requirements of the officer either in the first person or used the term the slave of the court (*banda-i dargāh*). A number of these first-person agreement forms survive in the Inayat Jang Collection of the National Archives, New Delhi.

227a **Acceptance of the Pledge (*Ta^cahhud*) for the Position of *Amīn* and *Faujdār*[1]**

I hereby accept with gratitude and zeal, the position of *amīn* and *faujdār* for ______ subdistrict, ______ district and province for the *maḥals* of *khāliṣa sharīf*, from the beginning of ______ to the end of ______ in accordance with the required one, two, or three year commitment. (I shall) remit the sum of ______ (amount) rupees *sikka mubārak* every year, without intermixing any crude or bad coins of whatever minting. (I shall not collect) anything other than the land revenue (*māl-o-jihāt*) and the proper cesses and allowances.

I affirm that upon confirmation of my appointment, I will convey in each season the stipulated installments of the aforesaid sum to the elevated *sarkār*. I promise that I will deduct the allowance for temporary revenue troops (*sih-bandī*) and for the *zamīndār's* assistance in collection (*nānkār*) etc. according to the scheduled rates for salary assignments (*jāgīrdārī*)[2] and the established custom (*ma^cmūl*).

If, God forbid, some natural calamity should occur, I will notify promptly the officers of the elevated *sarkār*. I shall deduct an allowance (from the stipulated installments) determined by the investigations of the present, trusted *amīn*, (the appointee). If such an extremity should blight the crops, I will sign an authorization for a (further) reduction in my pledged payments, after setting aside (previously) the allowances for *sih-bandī* etc. (as obtained) from the (current) total revenues. (I will calculate) the lost revenues (through crop damage) by setting alongside one another the investigations of the present *amīn*, as well as the original draft (*khām*) registers, the village accountant's (*paṭwārī*) papers, and the signed statements of the subdistrict headmen and accountants. I shall pay the remainder of that pledge to the final *dām*.

I have accordingly written these words of acceptance to serve henceforth as a warrant.[3]

Notes

1 The *ta'ahhud* is defined by Habib as "a pledge given by a prospective official about the amount he would assess or collect." *The Agrarian System*, p. 278. In general, however, as Habib points out, "the difference between the amount of the *ta'ahhud* and the actual revenue collected was not recoverable," i.e. by imperial practice.

2 The meaning of *jāgīrdārī* in this context is not at all certain.

3 The text concludes in the normal fashion, but an additional sentence is appended: "The *kharīf* was four installments; the *rabī^c* four installments." This phrase could simply refer to the schedule of payments referred to in the text: in the autumn or winter crop season four payments; in the spring season, four payments.

227b
Position of Administrator of Surat, the Auspicious Port

At this time, according to the exalted order, the position of administrator (*mutaṣaddī*) of Surat, the Auspicious Port, included within the province of Ahmadabad, the Jewel of Countries is transferred from ______ and conferred upon ______ from the beginning of ______, according to the details specified on the reverse of this document. The recipient must fulfill the duties and customary obligations of that position.

He must (continually) scrutinize all local accounts and affairs, and investigate the demands made by the collectors (*ᶜummāl*). If this examination reveals the collector of a fiscal unit to be dishonest and a wrongdoer, he should report his particulars to His Resplendent Majesty, so that another person may be appointed in his place.

He must exert every effort to punish malefactors and rebels, to destroy the strongholds of that group, to protect and succour the subjects and the local aristocracy, and to prevent smiths from manufacturing firearms. He should order the *thānadārs* (military commanders of fortified posts) whom he appoints to keep order and to seize nothing in the form of forbidden taxes.

No one may indulge in forbidden articles and intoxicants.

If malefactors of any village among those villages have become unruly and seditious, he must seize a number of them. He should then attempt to reform them so that they repent their stubborn and refractory ways, agree to pay their taxes, and submit to authority.

However, if due to their inherent deceitful villainy, these persons do not reform, he may attack that village and punish the malefactors. In so doing he should not molest the smaller cultivators. From any plunder which he may seize, such as livestock, etc. he may confiscate a penalty for the state equal to the proper land revenue demand for the aforesaid village.

He must guard the royal roads so that travellers and wayfarers may move back and forth with composed and tranquil minds. Nowhere may he
228a permit theft and highway robbery. In the event that the property of any person is lost by theft, he must recover those goods when capturing the thieves and highwaymen, and return the goods to their (rightful) owner. He must punish that band of miscreants. If he cannot recover the property, he must reimburse the owner for the value of the aforesaid goods.

He must exert every effort to expand the cultivated area; to resettle the peasants, and promote their welfare and tranquility; and to assess and collect the proper revenues for the royal lands (*khāliṣa sharīf*). He should apportion half (the agricultural produce) to the peasant, and half, without diminution, to the exalted state. He must order the collectors (*karoṛīyān*) to hand over to the treasurer the proceeds of the assessed land revenues. He may collect the additional sum of five rupees per hundred (of the current revenues) against the past years' arrears from the demarcated villages. He must also deposit (those sums) in the treasury. He (the

administrator) must vigilantly protect the revenues of the exalted state from the embezzling grasp of the collectors and treasurers. He must guard the treasury and recover from the cashkeepers and treasurers any amount outstanding from the revenue proceeds. He must remove (these funds) from their charge, have the funds deposited in the general treasury, and have a receipt made out. From the fees allotted to the collectors, he must withhold one rupee per hundred in anticipation of any future audit. He may pay the remainder of the aforesaid fees from the funds collected for arrears and agricultural loans, in accordance with the individual (*sanad*) issued by His Resplendent Majesty. If the aforesaid money is not sufficient to meet the cost of the collectors' allowances, he
228b may pay the necessary amount from the proceeds of the current year. He must collect by the regulation system (*ẕabṭ*) the established revenue proceeds of the ports. He should treat the merchants (of that port) with consideration.

When the harvest season ends he must use the record papers to investigate any embezzlement and fraud by the collectors (*ᶜummāl*). He should require them to repay whatever they owe (that appears in their names). He must protect the share (of the revenue) of the holy port of Surat.

The collectors, the *chaudhurīs*, the *qānūngos*, the village headmen, the cultivators, and the peasants of that place must accept the aforementioned person as administrator of that port. They must heed his prudent speech and righteous conduct provided that he attends to the interests of the exalted state and the prosperity of the peasants and rural aristocracy as specified on the reverse of this document. They must attend to his praise or complaint about themselves.

228b

Position of *Dīwān* of the Army

At this time, according to the exalted order, the position of *dīwān* of the army commanded by ______ is conferred upon ______. In fulfilling the duties and customary obligations of that position with rectitude and propriety, he (the latter) must not permit the slightest matter to escape his vigilance and care.

He must collect in the treasury of the army the monies intended for payment of the soldiers' salaries and for other salary headings (accounts) and secure these under his seal. After inspection of (those troops) present (at the muster) he may pay the salaries in conformity with the order of His Resplendent Majesty. And he must not permit the expenditure of a single *dām* without verified authorization from the *dīwān*. Otherwise, he will
229a have to repay and account for such sums.

As required by regulations and custom, he must send the income and expenditure accounts, treasury balances,[1] and other account papers, to the exalted office.

He should conduct himself properly (agreeably) with the clerks, staff, and salary claimants. He may not tyrannize over his subordinates.

(They) must accept the aforementioned person as *dīwān* of the aforesaid army and recognize that the duties and customary rights of that position belong to him.

Notes

1 The term is *arsaṭh* (also *arsaṭṭā*), cf. John T. Platts, *A Dictionary of Urdu, Classical Hindi, and English* (Oxford, 1930 edition, 1960 reprint), p. 40, a Hindi term meaning primarily cash accounts or a record of daily cash flow.

229a

Position of *Amīn* of *Pāybāqī*[1]

At this time, the position of *amīn* of *pāybāqī* lands, of estates recalled from religious beneficiaries (*a'imma*), and of subsistence lands exempted from taxation (*madad-ma*ᶜ*āsh*) in ______ subdistrict, ______ province, is transferred from ______ and conferred upon ______, according to the (stipulations) of the reverse, from the beginning of ______. He (the recipient) must fulfill the duties and customary obligations of that position with rectitude and propriety. He must treat the peasantry with consideration.

He must bring those *maḥals* (fiscal units, usually subdistricts) recalled into *pāybāqī*, into the regulation system correctly and definitively, that they may provide the salaries of the assignment holders (*jāgīrdārs*). He must assess the value (*jama*ᶜ) of those lands after scrutinizing the assessments for past years, made by the agents of previous *jāgīrdārs*, and after informing himself accurately of the existing (economic) conditions. He should then allot half (the produce) to the peasant and half to the exalted state.

He must require the collector (*karoṛī*) to deliver the revenue proceeds into the charge of the treasurer.

If, from time to time, the assessment of any single *maḥal* becomes outdated he must fix that unit's current assessment, and cause the proper revenue to be collected.

Every harvest season he must collect the extra sum of five rupees per hundred rupees of the current assessment from the villages, this additional sum to be applied to clear the outstanding arrears and balance of loans to the peasants. In the first installment of the current year's collections, he should take in that money loaned (*taqāwī*) to the peasants
229b in the previous year.

He must make every effort to expand the cultivated and settled areas.

He must recognize by the fixed rules and his own bond, his personal responsibility for the funds deposited with the treasurer. He (the *amīn*) must repay any amount outstanding in his name from the land revenue or from the stores.

He must ensure that not a single *dām* is spent without an authentic warrant from the *dīwān*. He should despatch all the funds in his charge to the general treasury, providing a receipt to the (local) treasurer. He must take care to reconcile his totals of the revenue collections with the amounts collected by the *jāgīrdār's* agents, leaving not even a single *dām* in arrears. He will be held accountable for any delayed transactions or uncollected arrears.

He must issue a receipt, bearing his seal and the signature of the treasurer, to the peasants for the money they pay the treasury. When all revenue in arrears has been paid in full, he may use those same receipts to compute the total revenue collected.

Save for the proper taxes he must not collect any of the forbidden levies.

He should hold back from the revenue collectors' allowances one rupee (per hundred) against any future audit. He should enter the amount withheld in the revenue assessment (*jama*ᶜ), so that he can explain (account for) that sum in the audit. He may pay the remainder of the aforesaid allowance to the collectors in conformity with each one's individual order (*sanad*), from the collected revenue arrears and loan repayments. If the aforementioned money is not sufficient to pay the collectors' allowances, he may pay the additional amount from the collections of the current year.

He must send the account papers to the exalted office according to regulations.

The *chaudhurīs* and *qānūngos*, the village headmen, the cultivators, and the peasants of that place must accept that position as belonging to the
230a aforementioned person. They must recognise his contract (*qaul-o-qarār*), assessments (*tashkhīs*), and authority as approved and valid. They must heed his prudent speech and righteous conduct. And they must attend to his praise or blame about themselves.

Notes

1 *Pāybāqī* lands were those villages or subdistricts administered temporarily by agents of the central administration pending reassignment to pay the salaries of other Mughal officers (*manṣabdārs*). Cf. Habib, *The Agrarian System*, p. 259n.

230a

Position of Revenue Collector (*Karoṛī*) of *Pāybāqī Maḥals*, of Estates Recalled from Religious Beneficiaries (*A'imma*) and Tax-exempt Land Grants (*Madad-Ma*ᶜ*āsh*)

The position of revenue collector for *maḥals* of *pāybāqī*, for estates recalled from religious beneficiaries, and for the lands (partially) exempted from taxation in ______ subdistrict, ______ district and province, in conformity with the details specified upon the reverse of this document, is conferred upon ______ from the beginning of ______. He must fulfill the duties and customary obligations of that position with rectitude and propriety. He must treat the peasantry with consideration.

He must bring those *maḥals* recalled into *pāybāqī*, into the regulation system, to provide the correct and definitive salaries of assignment holders. He (the *karorī*) must collect the fixed and proper total revenue that the *amīn*, with his advice, has assessed. (The *amīn's* determination is based upon) careful scrutiny of the revenue demanded in past years by agents of previous *jāgīrdārs*, and full knowledge of existing conditions. He must deliver whatever he collects to the treasurer. If any *maḥal* has not yet been assessed, he may make collections from that (unit) upon the advice of the *amīn*.

Every harvest season he must collect an extra five rupees per hundred of the current revenue demand for the villages, this additional sum to be applied against any arrears and balances of loans to the peasants. In the current year's first collections, he should include that money loaned to the peasants in the previous year. He must take great care to reconcile these (his returns) with those of the agents of the *jāgīrdārs*, leaving not a single
230b *dām* in arrears. He will be held accountable for any delayed transactions and remaining arrears. He must issue a receipt, bearing his seal and the signature of the treasurer, for the money that the peasants pay to the treasury. When the revenue collections in arrears have been paid in full, he may use those same receipts to compute the total revenue collected.

He must collect only the proper taxes, and not any forbidden levies.

He should hold back from his revenue collection allowance one rupee per hundred against any future audit. He should enter this in the revenue assessment (*jama*^{c}) so that he can explain (account for) that sum during the audit. He may take the remainder of the aforesaid allowance, in conformity with his individual order (*sanad*) and with the approval of the *amīn*, from the collected arrears and loan repayments. If the aforementioned money is not sufficient to pay the collector's allowance, he may take the necessary amount from the collections of the current year.

He must send the account papers to the exalted office according to regulations.

The *chaudhurīs* and *qānūngos*, the village headmen, the cultivators, and the peasants of that place must recognize the aforementioned person as the collector of those *maḥals*, and the duties and customary rights of that position as belonging to him.

230b

Order for the Position of Abolisher of Forbidden Beliefs (*Raf*^{c}*-i Abwāb-i Mamnū*^{c})[1]

The responsible officers of the Jewel of Countries, Ahmadabad Province, are hereby informed: at this time, according to the exalted order, the position of abolisher of forbidden beliefs, attached to the aforesaid province, is transferred from ______ and conferred upon ______. He (the

appointee) must fulfill the duties and customary obligations of that position with rectitude and propriety. He must not permit the slightest matter to escape his vigilance and care. He must act as strictly as is necessary to abolish forbidden beliefs, according to the commandments
231a of the resplendent Holy Law. He should appoint an orthodox prayer leader (*imām*) and an orthodox caller to prayer (*mu'azzin*) for the *masjid* built by the *Ismāʿīlī* sect (*qaum*). He must see that forbidden articles and intoxicating liquors are not used. He must take a bond from that sect (*farīq*) that they now repudiate the deranged claims of those people (the *Ismāʿīlī* leaders).

The aforesaid position is hereby conferred upon the aforementioned person. The duties and customary rights of that position belong to him. They are to know that there are strict injunctions in this matter.

Notes

1 This particular office reflects the Emperor Aurangzeb's continuing effort to stamp out *Ismāʿīlī* activities in Gujarat. The compiler of the *Mir'āt-i Aḥmadī* reported that the Emperor summoned Sayyid Shahji, a wealthy and popular *Ismāʿīlī* spiritual leader living in Ahmadabad, to the imperial court *circa* 1100 A.H./A.D. 1688–89. The subsequent death of the Sayyid by suicide touched off a massive series of revolts by his followers. The Governor of Ahmadabad Province suppressed these only with much effort and bloodshed. Thereafter imperial officers continued to press the members of this sect very hard to abandon their unorthodox beliefs and allegiance for the remainder of Aurangzeb's reign. See Ali Muhammad Khan, *Mir'āt-i Aḥmadī*, pp. 286–289, and Aniruddha Ray, "Francis Martin's Account of the Rising of the Matiyas in 1685," in *Proceedings of the Indian History Congress* (1969): 195–203.

231a Charge-Order (*Sanad-i Sipurd*) to Defray the Expenses of Special Robes of Honor[1] (*Malbūs-i khāṣṣ*)

At this time, according to the exalted order, the sum of ______ (amount) *dāms* (assessed revenue) from ______ subdistrict, ______ district and province, which upon the transfer of ______ has been recalled into the temporary pool of lands awaiting assignment (*pāybāqī*) in the *khāliṣa sharīf*. From the beginning of ______ this (revenue) has been placed in the charge[2] of that most noble person to defray expenses for special robes of honor (*malbūs-i khāṣṣ*). He must make a strenuous effort to increase the population, to extend the cultivated area, to expand the revenue collections of the exalted state, and to preserve the tranquility of the peasantry.

Having acquired this allowance from the revenue proceeds, he must prepare the special robes of honor in conformity with the requirements of the purchasing establishment (*ibtiyāʿkhāna*). He must send them (the robes) to His Resplendent Majesty. They are to know that there are strict injunctions in this matter.

Notes

1 Cf. M. Athar Ali, *Mughal Nobility*, p. 140, for the term *malbūs-khāṣṣ*. The *khil'ats* or robes of honor were highly decorated dresses, girdles, and caps made of from three to seven separate pieces. The Emperor was usually the first person to wear these special robes, whether symbolically or actually, and he then presented them personally to the recipient. This presentation created a ritual bond between the Mughal throne and the *manṣabdār* who received the robes.

2 This phrase might also have a more technical meaning; the term translated as 'charge' is *ʿuhda*, meaning an obligation or responsibility, and a variant of *taʿahhud*, the pledge of the revenue collector (see folio 227a). Thus this officer may have had to collect all revenues from this territory as well as these special revenues.

231a Position of Highway Patrol Commander (*Rāhdār*) and Military Commander of a Fortified Post (*Thānadār*)

At this time the position of highway patrol commander, and fortified post command for ______ place included within ______ province is transferred from ______ and conferred upon ______ in conformity with the details specified on the reverse of this document. He (the appointee) must fulfill the duties and customary obligations of that position with rectitude and propriety. He must exert every effort to maintain order, to administer according to the regulations, to punish and chastise malefactors and rebels, to protect and succour both the smaller cultivators and larger taxpayers, and to prevent smiths from manufacturing firearms. He must take special care that no one uses forbidden articles or intoxicating drugs.
231b He must guard the royal roads so that travellers and wayfarers may move back and forth with composed and tranquil minds. He must eliminate all trace of thieves or highway robbers. If the property of any person is stolen or plundered, he must recover it when capturing the thieves and highwaymen, and return the goods to their (rightful) owner. He must punish that band of miscreants. If he cannot recover the property he must reimburse the owner for (the value of) the aforesaid goods.

The *chaudhurīs* and *qānūngos*, the *zamīndārs*, village headman, cultivators, and peasants of that place must accept the charge of highway patrol commander and post commander for that locality as conferred upon the aforementioned person. They must recognize that the duties and customary rights of that position belong to him.

231b Position of the *Īrmān* (Ruler) of the *Tūmān* (District) of *Peshāwar*

The responsible officers and regulators of affairs, present and future, the chiefs (*malikān*), headmen (*muqaddamān*), cultivators, and peasants of the *tūmān* of Peshāwar included within the *Dār al-mulk* Kābul are hereby informed: at this time, according to the exalted order, the position of *Īrmān* of the district of Peshāwar is transferred from ______ and conferred upon ______ in conformity with the details set out on the reverse of this document.

He (the recipient) must fulfill the duties and customary obligations of that (position) with rectitude and propriety. He must not permit the slightest matter to escape his vigilance and care.

He must do his utmost to administer correctly the revenues of that aforementioned district, and to safeguard the tranquility of the peasantry on the frontier (*marzbūm*). He must rely on no other person as his partner or associate.

Every year, he must deposit in the treasury of the aforesaid province (Kābul), an installment of five thousand rupees, toward a total of forty thousand rupees *peshkash* (tribute) for the exalted state, (to be paid in full) within eight years.

He may take the chief's allowances and the tax-exempt lands of the *Īrmān* (belonging to) his grandfather and father, but he must not desire or expect more than this.

The aforesaid position is conferred upon the aforementioned person and they (the officers) must recognize that the duties and customary
232a rights of that position belong to him. They must apportion the tax-exempt land grants, perquisites, *zamīndārs'* revenue collection allowances (*nānkār*), expenses for the royal table (*kharj alūshī*), revenue assessment, etc., of Peshāwar, in consultation with him.[1] They are to know that there are strict injunctions in this matter.

Notes

1 This listing of categories of allowances and revenues is extremely confused. Qureshi, in *The Administration of the Mughal Empire*, p. 237, cites the *Ā'īn-i Akbarī* of Abul Fazl for the basic administrative unit in Kabul province as a *tūmān*. From the time of Chingiz Khan, and before, the Mongols had utilized the decimal principle of army organization in which the largest single unit was the *tūmān* or 10,000 horsemen.

232a **Position of Superintendent of the *Dīwān*'s Office and Establishment (*Dārogha-i Kachahrī*)**

This order is issued to the responsible officers, functionaries, and staff of the *dīwān's* office (*kachahrī*) of ______ province: at this time, according to the exalted order, the position of superintendent of the aforementioned *kachaharī* is transferred from ______ and conferred upon ______. He (the appointee) must fulfill the duties and customary obligations of that position with rectitude and propriety. He must not allow the slightest matter to escape his vigilance and care. He must take care to prevent any loss or negligence in all transactions and affairs of that place.

He must prepare accurate copies of the account papers from the subdistricts (*parganāt*). After the provincial *dīwān* has scrutinized the accounts, the superintendent must ensure that they are sent each year to the sublime office (at the imperial capital). He (the superintendent), using extreme care, may collect and deposit in the provincial treasury (*khizāna-i ᶜāmira*) any officer's outstanding balance as established by treasury claims and accounts,[1] and certified by the provincial *dīwān*.

They (the officers mentioned) must accept the aforementioned person as *dārogha-i kachahrī*. They must recognize that the duties and customary rights of that position belong to him.

Notes

1 "*Mutālaba wa muhāsaba bāshad*" refers to the financial transactions ongoing between each imperial officer (*manṣabdār*) and the various imperial treasuries. Mughal officers often took treasury loans or advances against their salaries, or incurred fines for various infractions of regulations, and thus acquired fiscal obligations to the treasury. On the other hand, delayed salary payments or *jāgīr* assignments gave them a claim against the treasury. These various account balances were sorted out at periodic intervals, as well as at the death or retirement of the officer. For a more detailed explanation, *see* M. Athar Ali, *The Mughal Nobility*, pp. 51–53.

232a

Position of Superintendent of Grain Sales (*Dārogha-i Mubīᶜi Ghallāt*)

This order is issued to the responsible officers, clerks, and staff of ______ (place): at this time, the position of superintendent of grain sales is transferred from ______ and conferred upon ______. He (the appointee) must fulfill the duties and customary obligations of that position with
232b rectitude and propriety.

He should time the sale of grain to produce the maximum profit. He must deposit the money realized from that (sale) in charge of the cashkeeper (treasurer). He must not expand a single *dām* from (the funds under) his charge without an authentic warrant from the *dīwān*. He must have all the funds in his charge sent to the provincial treasury, from which he must obtain a receipt.

They (the officers mentioned) must accept the aforementioned person as superintendent of grain sales for that place and recognize that the duties and customary rights of that position belong to him.

232b

Position of Claims Settlement Officer (*Istīfā'*)

This order is issued to ______: at this time, the position of claims settlement officer of ______ is transferred from ______ and conferred upon him. He must fulfill all the duties and customary obligations of that position with rectitude and propriety. He must not let the slightest point of information escape him in examining the final accounts and the treasury claims. Having computed and settled the accounts according to the regulations, he must bring them to the *dīwān* of the province for his signature. Thereafter, in accordance with that (computation), he may exact the necessary deductions and demand restitution. They (the officers of that place) are to know that there are strict injunctions in this matter.

232b

Position of Secretary (*Peshkār*) to the *Dīwān* of the Army

This order is issued to the responsible officers, the clerks and staff of the *dīwān* of the army under the command of (*hamrāhī*) ______: at this time the position of secretary for the *dīwān* of the aforementioned army is conferred upon ______. He must fulfill the duties and customary obligations of that position with rectitude and propriety. He must not permit the slightest matter to escape his vigilance and care. He must be careful not to permit a single *dām* to be paid (to the army) from the money allocated for salaries (*tankhwāh*) or other types of claims in the army treasury, without an authentic warrant from the *dīwān* of the army.
233a He must scrutinize minutely all salary payments, recognizing his obligation under the regulations to investigate these (transactions) thoroughly.

In conformity with regulations, he must prepare corrected and detailed copies for the *dīwān* of the income and expense records, treasury balances, and other account papers and have these sent to the exalted office (at the imperial capital or camp).

Having treated the clerks and staff with consideration, he must carry out his tasks with integrity. They must recognize that the aforementioned position is conferred upon the aforesaid person and that the duties and customary rights of that position belong to him.

233a

Position of Superintendent and Assessor of *Sā'ir*

This is issued to the responsible officers, clerks, and staff of the *maḥals* of *sā'ir* of ______ province: at this time in accordance with the exalted order, the position of superintendent (*dārogha*) (or) assessor (*amīn*) of the aforementioned *maḥals* is transferred from ______ and conferred upon ______. He (the appointee) must fulfill the duties and customary obligations of that position with rectitude and propriety. He must not allow the slightest matter to escape his vigilance and care.

He should take in the proceeds of the two and one-half and five per cent[1] tax according to the established rules and deposit them with the treasurer. He should regard the protection and guarding of the funds in his (the treasurer's) custody as a personal obligation. He must not permit a single *dām* to be expended without an authentic warrant from the *dīwān*. He (the *amīn*) must be sure that all the funds in his custody arrive at the general treasury and that he obtains a full receipt. At night he must guard

the merchants' goods under his own seal and that of the superintendent (*dārogha*). He must repay from his allowance, according to the fixed rules, each *dām* from the proceeds of goods (sold) there that he may
233b deduct or divert for his own use. He must be extremely careful to prevent the Hindu traders from certifying their own goods under the names of Muslims. He should take a bond to that effect from the brokers of that place.

They (the officers mentioned above) must accept the aforementioned person as either the superintendent or the *amīn* of that place. They must recognize that the duties and customary rights of that position belong to him.

Notes

1 The Emperor Aurangzeb reimposed the canonical Islamic tax levied on the import and export of commodities in the twenty-fifth year of his reign. Muslim traders, as stated above, paid two and one-half per cent on value for commodities at the time and place of the original purchase. Hindus paid five per cent at the time of purchase, and Christians and Jews paid three and one-half per cent. *See* Qureshi, *The Administration of the Mughal Empire*, pp. 146–147, for a discussion of this practice.

233b In the Order (*Sanad*) for the Position of Collector of the Treasury[1]

This additional statement must be written: That he must vigilantly guard and patrol (*gird-awārī*) the transfer (importation) of monies from the stations, customs houses, and outlying areas, so that the flow of such funds may not be interrupted.

Notes

1 This section is apparently an addition for the letter given to a new treasury collector. See folio 237a below.

233b Falconry Order (*Dastak-ī Qūshkhāna*)

This order is issued in the names of the agents of the *faujdārs*, *jāgīrdārs*, customs officers (*guzarbānān*), and officers protecting the roads and highways: a document bearing the seal of the falconry officers of the exalted state (the Emperor) has arrived at the central office. (The document states) that those creatures (the falcons) under the care of ______, head falconers, have gone for moulting to ______ subdistrict. His Resplendent Majesty has ordered that: customs dues and road taxes must be set aside in every place where those officers may cause those hunting animals to alight. They (the local officers) must supply whatever may be demanded for (the falcons') food, such as small birds and minced meat, etc., without delay, or they may provide an allowance (of money) equivalent to the prevailing price of those (supplies).

Thus (the imperial officers) must take care that no one uses threats or force to make them (the falcons) alight at the residence of anyone. No assailant may harm or injure those creatures.

233b **Position of Assayer (*Chaukasī*) and Master Weigher (*Wazn-kash*) of the Mint**

234a This order is issued to the responsible officers, clerks and staff of the mint of ______ place: at this time the position of assayer and master weigher for gold and silver of the aforementioned *maḥals* is transferred from ______ and conferred upon ______. He (the appointee) must fulfill the duties and obligations of that position with rectitude and propriety. He must not permit the slightest matter to escape his vigilance and care.

He must try to satisfy the traders (*baipārīyān*) (who deal with the mint) completely and to create abundant proceeds for the exalted state. He must ensure that the *ashrafī* (gold coins) and rupees (silver coins) arrive at the required weight and the finest assay in conformity with the rules for the coin of current issue (*sikka mubārak*). According to practice, he may take eight *annas* for every one thousand rupees (struck) as his allowance (for the master weigher and assayer), but apart from that, he may demand nothing more.

They (the officers mentioned) must accept the aforementioned person as assayer and master weigher of the aforesaid *maḥals* and they must recognize that the duties and customary rights of that position belong to him.

234a **Position of Writer of Receipts for *Manṣabdārs* (*Qabẓ-nawīsī Manṣabdārān*)**

This order is issued to the responsible officers, clerks, and staff of the provincial treasury: at this time, the position of writer of receipts for the *manṣabdārs* of that place is transferred from ______ and conferred upon ______. He (the appointee) must completely fulfill the duties and customary obligations of that position. He must not allow the slightest matter to escape his care and vigilance.

He must send the *manṣabdārs'* receipts to the exalted office according to regulations.

They (the officers mentioned) must accept the aforementioned person as writer of receipts for the *manṣabdārs* of that place. They must recognize that the duties and customary rights of that position belong to him.

234a **Position of *Amīn* for Payment of Stipends to Daily Pensioners, etc.**

234b This order is issued to the officers of the *sā'ir maḥals* of the Royal Grain Market and the Market of the Stirrup, etc., located within the royal capital at Delhi, and with the Stirrup of Felicity (the imperial camp): at this time the position of *amīn* for payment of cash stipends to the daily, monthly, and yearly pensioners of that place is transferred from ______ and conferred upon ______. He must fulfill the duties and customary obligations of that (position) with rectitude and propriety. He must not allow the slightest matter to escape his vigilance and care.

He should draw the funds for the stipends of that group from the officers of the aforesaid *maḥals*. He may make cash payments (to the pensioners) after verifying the authenticity of the grants, the sanctity of their persons, and the presence of the provincial *dīwān's* seal on their payment orders in accordance with regulations. He (the *amīn*) must obtain a receipt bearing the seal of each recipient. He (the *amīn*) must despatch, for each year, the (accounts of) total expenditures for that (purpose) to the exalted office.

They (the above mentioned officers) must accept the aforementioned *khān* as *amīn* for payment of cash stipends. They must recognize that the duties and customary right of that (position) belong to him.

234b **Master of the Docks and Superintendent of the Salt Works of the Port**

This order is issued to the responsible officers of Surat, the Auspicious Port, included within the province of Ahmadabad: at this time, according to the exalted order, the position of master of the docks and superintendent of the salt works of the aforementioned port is transferred from ______ and conferred upon ______. He (the appointee) must fulfill the duties and customary obligations of that position with rectitude and propriety. He must not permit the slightest matter to escape his vigilance
235a and care. He must treat the merchants, etc., with consideration.

He must take all necessary precautions in collecting the revenues of the exalted state. He should also take care to prevent any omission or neglect in the affairs of that place.

They (the officers mentioned) must accept the aforementioned as master of the docks and superintendent of the salt works of that place. They must recognize that the duties and customary rights of that position belong to him.

235a **Position of Harbor Master and Superintendent of Boats (*Mīr-baḥrī wa Dārogha-i Nawāra*)**[1]

This order is issued to the responsible officers, clerks, and staff under the harbor master of ______ place: at this time, according to the exalted order, the position of harbor master of that place is transferred from ______ and conferred upon ______. He must fulfill the duties and customary obligations of that position with rectitude and propriety. He must not allow the slightest matter to escape his vigilance and concern.

He must protect the ships (*kashtīhā*) carefully at nightfall. He must use the utmost vigilance to ensure that none of the malefactors and rebels are able (to board the ships) and cross over.

They must accept the aformentioned person as harbor master of that place. They must recognize that the duties and customary rights of that position belong to him.

Notes

1 Cf. I. H. Qureshi, *The Administration of the Mughal Empire*, p. 231: "The provincial *mīr baḥr* was responsible for the maintenance of the river and sea ports within his jurisdiction in good condition, to guard and supervise river communications and to keep the *nawwārah* in good order." The Mughals used the term *nawāra* for the various imperial fleets employed for military and patrolling purposes in Bengal and other coastal provinces. These fleets were composed of both riverine and coastal craft, equipped with both oars and sails. The *mir baḥrī* could also, depending upon the context, be a high-ranking officer placed in charge of a war fleet. This role was especially critical in the long-drawn-out Mughal expansion into Bengal between A.D. 1570 and 1670. *See* Atul Chandra Roy, *A History of Mughal Navy and Naval Warfares* (Calcutta, 1972), for a detailed treatment of Mughal naval organization, ships and boats, and administration.

235a

Position of *Amīn* of the City Magistrate's Office

This order is issued to the responsible officers, clerks, and staff of the magistrate's office of ______ city: according to the exalted order, the position of *amīn* of the office of the aforesaid magistrate is transferred from ______ and conferred upon ______. He (the appointee) must fulfill the duties and customary obligations of that position with rectitude and propriety. He should not permit the slightest matter to escape his vigilance and care. He should conduct himself properly with the clerks and staff of that place. He must take special care to prevent any omission
235b or neglect in the affairs of that place. They must accept the aforementioned as *amīn* of that place and recognize that the duties and customary rights of that (position) belong to him.

235b

Position of Secretary (*Peshkār*) to the *Dīwān* of the Province

This order is issued to the responsible officers, clerks and staff of the *dīwān's* office of ______ province: according to the exalted order, the position of secretary of the *dīwān's* office of the aforesaid province, is transferred from ______ and conferred upon ______. He must fulfill the duties and customary obligations of that position with rectitude and propriety. He must not allow the slightest matter to escape his vigilance and care. He is to prepare the account papers for the *dīwān's* office of the aforesaid province according to regulations. He must despatch the *dīwān's* copies, the salary claim papers, etc., for each year to the central office in conformity with the fixed rules. He must take great care to prevent any omission or neglect in transacting the affairs of that place.

They must accept that aforementioned person as secretary to the *dīwān's* office of the aforesaid province. And they must recognize that the duties and customary rights of that (position) belong to him.

235b Position of Supervisor and Captain of Ships (*Nākhudā*) for the Port of Surat

This order is issued to the responsible officers and those entrusted with the management of affairs, the clerks and staff of the Port of Holy Surat, the Jewel of Countries, Ahmadabad province: at this time, according to the exalted order, the position of supervisor and captain of ships for the exalted state, assigned to the aforesaid port, is transferred from ______ and conferred upon ______ in conformity with the details set out on the reverse of this document. He (the appointee) must attend to the duties and customary obligations of that position with rectitude and propriety, reliably and honestly. He must not permit the slightest matter to escape
236a his vigilance and care. He must conduct himself properly with the clerks and staff of that place.

The aforementioned positions having been assigned to the charge of the aforesaid person, they (the officers mentioned) must recognize that the duties and customary rights of that position belong to him. Moreover, they must follow his orders in executing the business of that place.

236a Position of Superintendent (*Dārogha*) of the Treasury

This order is issued to the responsible officers, clerks and staff of the treasury of ______ province: at this time, according to the exalted order, the position of superintendent of the aforesaid treasury is transferred from ______ and conferred upon ______. He (the appointee) must fulfill the duties and customary obligations of that position with rectitude and propriety. He must not permit the slightest matter to escape his vigilance and care.

Having truly protected the treasury, he must inform himself fully so as to prevent any discrepancy between payments and withdrawals. He must not expend a single *dām* without an authentic certificate from the *dīwān*. He should secure the accumulated money in the vault of the treasury, and then lock the vault and seal it with his seal and that of the treasurer. Only in his own (the superintendent's) presence may it (the vault) be opened or closed. He must be extremely careful to repel any attempt at embezzlement.

They (the officers mentioned) must accept the aforementioned person as superintendent of the aforesaid treasury. And they must recognize that the duties and customary rights of that position belong to him.

236a Position of Headman (*Chaudhurī*) of the Money Changers' Market (*Ṣarrāfa*)[1]

This order is issued to the responsible officers, clerks, and staff of the money changers' market of ______ city: at this time, the position of headman of the money changers' market of the aforesaid city is transferred from ______ and conferred upon ______. He (the appointee) must
236b fulfill the duties and customary obligations of this position with rectitude and propriety. He must not permit the slightest matter to escape his vigilance and care.

He must send to the officers of that place a memorandum of the best market purchase price for silver coin.

He should gratify the clerks and staff of that place by his proper conduct. He should not demand from the money changers (*ṣarrāfān*) anything other than his established customary dues, and he should not introduce new or forbidden exactions.

They must accept the aforementioned person as headman of the money changers' market of the aforesaid city. And they must recognize that the duties and customary rights of that belong to him. They may not exceed the bounds of prudent speech, appropriate behavior and righteous conduct with him while he is attending to the prosperity of the exalted state and the tranquillity of the populace.

Notes

1 The *ṣarrāf*, here translated as money changer, played an indispensable role in the economy of Mughal India. Usually Hindu and members of a regional trading caste, the *ṣarrāfs* (English corruption 'shroff') provided a money-changing service for all comers. They accepted Manila dollars, South Indian gold *hūn* (pagodas), or any of dozens of foreign and indigenous coins in exchange for equivalent Mughal rupees, current issue acceptable at official treasuries, or for any other desired currency. The exchange rate was determined by prevailing market conditions, the condition of the proferred coins, and by the small service charge made by the money changer. *Ṣarrāfs* also took coin and bullion to the Mughal provincial mint and paid to have this melted and struck in silver or gold currency which they returned to circulation. In return for a small discount the *ṣarrāfs* offered bills of exchange (*hunḍī*), usually payable within two months to the bearer, and saleable. These could be used to despatch money from one city or town to another. The exchange or *ṣarrāfat* of money changers organized in one urban center balanced off accounts with other collectivities of *ṣarrāfs* in order to operate this system. Finally, the *ṣarrāfs* offered credit for commerce, for administration or

any other purposes, either by straight loans or by use of *huṇḍīs*. For an enlarged description of the role of the *ṣarrāf*, *see* Irfan Habib, "Banking in Medieval India," in Tapan Raychaudhuri, ed., *Contributions to Indian Economic History*, 1 (1960): 8–14, and "Usury in Medieval India," *Comparative Studies in Society and History* (1964): 393–419. Habib has revised some of his earlier views in an essay on "The System of Bills of Exchange (Hundīs) in the Mughal Empire," in *Proceedings of the Indian History Congress* (1972): 209–303.

236b **Position of Accountant (*Mushrif*) of a Subdistrict**

This order is issued to the responsible officers of ______ subdistrict (*pargana*), of ______ district and ______ province: at this time the position of accountant of the aforesaid subdistrict is transferred from ______ and conferred upon ______. He (the appointee) must fulfill the duties and customary obligations of that position with rectitude and propriety. He must not permit the slightest matter to escape his vigilance and care.

He must prepare the account papers of that place in conformity with fixed regulations and established rules so that any future investigation (or audit) will not reveal any discrepancy or surplus. He must despatch (those records) to the exalted office (the office of the provincial *dīwān*).

He must not pay a salary to anyone from the funds in charge of the cashkeeper of that place without an authentic warrant from the *dīwān*. If (he does) so, he will be personally responsible (to answer for that sum).

He must conduct himself properly so as to gratify the clerks and staff and he must display the utmost integrity in fulfilling the requirements of
237a this position. They must accept the aforementiond person as accountant of that place. They must recognize that the duties and customary rights of that position belong to him.

237a **Collector for the Treasury and Transmittal Officer (*Sazāwal*) for Cash Installments of the *Pargana***

This order is issued in the names of the responsible officers, clerks, and staff of ______ subdistrict, and ______ district and ______ province: at this time, the position of collector and transmittal officer for cash installments of the aforesaid subdistrict is transferred from ______ and conferred upon ______. He (the appointee) must fulfill the duties and customary obligations of this position with rectitude and propriety. He must not permit the slightest matter to escape his vigilance and care. He must protect the treasury so as to avoid any discrepancy between income and expenditure. He must not allow a single *dām* or *dirham* to be spent without an authentic warrant from the *dīwān*. He must send, without any delay, the cash installments of the subdistrict to His Resplendent Majesty.

They (the officers mentioned) must accept the aforementioned person as collector of the treasury and transmittal officer for the cash installments of the aforesaid subdistrict. They must recognize that the duties and customary rights of this position belong to him.

237a **Position of News Writer (*Akhbār-nawīs*) for the Subdistrict**

This order is issued to ______: at this time the position of news writer of ______ subdistrict is transferred from ______ and conferred upon ______. He (the appointee) must fulfill the duties and customary obligations of that (position) with complete rectitude and propriety. He must not permit the slightest matter to escape his vigilance and care.

He must inform himself of the transactions and events of the aforesaid subdistrict in detail, with complete profundity and accuracy. He must prepare copies of the news reports free of any discrepancy, abridgement, or
237b deletion. He must prepare them so as to prevent any omission or neglect. He must send these copies to His Resplendent Majesty. He is to know that there are strict injunctions in this matter.

237b **Position of Superintendent (*Dārogha*) of the Treasury and Transmittal Officer (*Sazāwal*) for Provincial Records**

This order is issued to the responsible officer of ______ province: at this time, according to the exalted order, the position of superintendent of the treasury and transmittal officer for provincial records for the aforesaid province, is transferred from ______ and conferred upon ______. He (the appointee) must fulfill the duties and customary obligations of that (position) with rectitude and propriety. He must not allow the slightest matter to escape his vigilance and care. In accordance with fixed regulations and established rules, and in cooperation with the *dīwān* of the province and the *amīn* (of the treasury), he must deposit in the treasury the accumulated revenue proceeds of the subdistricts, treasury claims against *jāgīrdārs* (*muṭālabāt*), and other taxes and cesses (taxes other than revenue). He is to lock the door of the treasury and secure it with his own seal. It must be opened and closed (only) in his presence.

He must take special care to repel any attempt at embezzlement or fraud. He may expend nothing without an authentic warrant from the *dīwān*.

Every fifteen days in conformity with the rules, he must send to His Resplendent Majesty the account papers showing the treasury balances. He must ensure that the revenue collectors of the reserved lands of that province (*ʿummāl-ī maḥāl-ī khāliṣa sharīf*) prepare the current revenue assessment (*daul-jamaʿ*), the summary of revenue proceeds and arrears (*wāṣilbāqī*), and other account papers according to fixed regulations and established rules. He should send these (records first for) scrutiny to the provincial *dīwān*, and thereafter to the central office without delay or procrastination.

They (the officers mentioned) must accept the aforementioned person as superintendent of the treasury and transmittal officer for provincial records of that place, in conformity with the imperial mandate (*yarlīgh*).

237b
238a

Position of Record Keeper (*Mushrif*) of the Magistrate's Gaol (*Paṇḍit-khāna Chabūtara*)

This order is issued to the responsible officers, clerks, and staff, of the magistrate's office of the Stirrup of Felicity (the imperial camp) or to the capital, *Dār al-khilāfat, Shāhjahānābād* (Delhi): at this time, the position of recond keeper for the gaol of the aforesaid establishment is transferred from ______ and conferred upon ______. He (the appointee) must fulfill completely the duties and customary obligations of this position. He must not permit the slightest matter to escape his vigilance and care.

In conformity with regulations, he must maintain the official records showing for each prisoner the cause of imprisonment and the reason for discharge.

They (the officers mentioned) must accept him as record keeper of the gaol and recognize that the duties and customary rights of that position belong to him.

238a

Position of Head Mace-Bearer (*Mīr-dah*) (or) Head Staff-Bearer (*Danḍī*) (or) Head Bailiff (*Nāẓir*)[1]

This order is issued to the responsible officers, clerks and staff of ______ (place): at this time the position of head mace-bearer, head staff-bearer, or head bailiff of that place is transferred from ______ and conferred upon ______. He (the appointee) must fulfill the duties and customary obligations (of that position) with rectitude and propriety. He must not permit the slightest matter to escape his vigilance and care.

He must ensure that the footmen assigned to that place are on duty and fully attentive in the royal work.

They must accept the aforementioned person as head mace-bearer, head staff-bearer, or head bailiff of that place. They must recognize that the duties and customary rights of that position belong to him.

Notes

1 All three terms referred to the commanders of small bodies of armed footmen used by the imperial administration as guards and attendants at various public audiences, for the law courts, etc. These men were not really soldiers nor utilized as such. They also carried important messages and summons for the higher-ranking provincial officers. The appearance of mace-bearers sent directly from the Emperor at the camp or office of a provincial governor or other officer was a notable, but frequently ominous, occasion for the recipient. The

imperial mace-bearers, wearing brocaded robes and carrying either gold or silver maces, were supposed to be received as directly representing the Emperor's person. However, apparently less awesome mace-bearers served in more mundane capacities under provincial governors and *dīwāns*. In A.D. 1694, for example, a rebellious *zamīndār* captured a mace-bearer carrying cash for the treasury of Ganjikota fort in Hyderabad province. The *zamīndār* held the mace-bearer for ransom for two months. Cf. Richards, *Mughal Administration in Golconda*, pp. 119–120.

238a **According to the Exalted Order in the Name of the Governor of Bengal Province (after writing the titles)**

At this time, ______, etc., bankers (*sāhūān*), in conformity with the standing order, have placed the sum of ______ *lakh* (amount, in hundreds of thousands of rupees) in the general treasury of the Stirrup of Felicity (the Emperor's court or camp).[1] As compensation for this aforesaid amount, of ______ (amount) rupees, and for the expense for discount on a bill of exchange (*huṅḍāwan*)[2] and gratuities (*inᶜām*) fixed at three months, payment has been ordered from the treasury of the Paradise of
238b Countries, Bengal. Therefore according to the sublime elevated order, let the person holding the dignity of authority and governance make this payment speedily when he has received the order (*parwāna*) from His Resplendent Majesty issued in the name of the *dīwān* of the province. They are to know that the Refuge of Mankind (the Emperor) has imposed strict injunctions in this matter.

Notes

1 This standard order was probably used for the transfer of the surplus revenues from Bengal to the central treasury. From A.D. 1700 on, after Murshid Qulī Khān was assigned to Bengal as provincial *dīwān* and had reorganized the provincial administration, the Bengal surplus became the financial mainstay of the Emperor Aurangzeb and his immediate successors. By A.D. 1702 Murshid Qulī Khān was sending an annual sum of ten million silver rupees to the Emperor – an extraordinary amount in view of the rural unrest and therefore plummeting revenues elsewhere in the Mughal empire at this time. Murshid Qulī Khān continued to remit enormous sums to the centre from Bengal until his death in A.D. 1727. However, this order does reveal one apparent discrepancy with what is known of the usual mode of remittance. The cost of bills of exchange would have been prohibitive, even if possible, for such large sums, and the *dīwān* therefore had the treasure, in silver coin, delivered to Delhi by a large convoy of bullock-drawn carts, under heavy military escort. Apart from this treasure shipment however, it is possible that the Bengal authorities purchased bankers' bills (*huṇḍīs*) to transfer additional or supplemental amounts to the Emperor's treasury. *See* Jadunath Sarkar, ed., *History of Bengal, Muslim Period* (Patna, 1973 reprint ed.), pp. 397–421. *See also* Mehta Balmukund, *Letters of a King-Maker of the Eighteenth Century*, edited and translated by Satish Chandra, (Aligarh, 1972), p. 39, for two letters sent by the imperial *wazīr* to Murshid Qulī Khān in 1720: the first, a reply to a report sent by Murshid Qulī Khān, commended him for personally "escorting

90 *lakhs* of treasure [nine million silver rupees] which had been loaded in carts (up to a distance of) two *kos* from the city; [and for] the appointment of Faiyyaz Ali Khan, the *bakhshi* of the *ṣūbah* [chief military officer of the province] to accompany it with your troops."

2 The usual term for a bill of exchange is *huṇḍī*, originally a Hindi word derived from the Sanskrit. *Huṅḍāwan*, the term used here, denotes the rate or price paid for a bill, that is the discount itself. Cf. Platts' *Dictionary*, p. 1237.

238b

According to the Exalted Order in the Name of the *Dīwān* of Bengal (after writing the titles)

At this time, ______ etc., bankers, in conformity with the standing order, have placed the sum of ______ *lakh* (amount, in hundreds of thousands of rupees) in the general treasury of the Stirrup of Felicity (the Emperor's camp). In compensation for this aforesaid amount of ______ rupees and the expense for discount on a bill of exchange and gratuities fixed at three months, payment has been ordered from the treasury of the Paradise of Countries, Bengal.[1] Therefore, let the most wise one (the *dīwān*) pay the aforesaid amount after deducting two *surkh*[2] in accordance with the details stipulated on the reverse.

He is to obtain a receipt bearing the seals of the bankers.

Henceforth he is to set aside as an allowance and enumerate on current account this same order (*parwāna*) and receipt (*qabẓ al-wuṣūl*). He is to know that there are strict injunctions in this matter.

Notes

1 See notes for previous order.

2 The meaning of this phrase is unclear. *Surkh* is a synonym for the *rattī*, a jeweler's and banker's weight equal to just under two English grains in the Mughal period. Steingass' Dictionary uses the same term in its other meaning, to refer simply to gold (in any amount).

238b

Order for the Cultivation of Long-untilled Land (*Banjar*) Under the Regulation for Reduced Revenues[1]

The responsible officers, present and future of ______ subdistrict, ______ district and ______ province are hereby informed that: at this time ______ has testified that the amount of waste land no longer assessable is very great in the aforesaid subdistrict, and has requested that this quantity of *bīgha* from that total may be entrusted to this slave under the regulation for reduced assessment. In return, he will sow the lands and will cause an appropriate revenue to be returned from those lands assessed at the reduced rate. He intends to promote the contentment of the populace and the settlement of that verdant country under the
239a Sublime and Resplendent Gaze (of the Emperor).

Therefore it is laid down that so many *bīgha* from the land which has fallen out of cultivation and is outside the assessment, provided that the owner is not present, or if present is unable (to cultivate it), shall be transferred to the aforementioned person so that he shall, as far as he is able, cultivate the land and pay the following rate of tax: in the first year, one-fifth part; in the second year, one-fourth part; and in the third year, one-third part (of the total harvest). They (the officers) are not to trouble (him) in any way for other revenue, cesses or expenses.

They (the officers) must be careful not to apply the deduction for long-untilled waste lands fallen out of assessment to lands already cultivated. If future investigation reveals such a violation, they must recall and recover one half (the produce) up to the full rate of collection for sown lands. (The amount recovered must be calculated) from the date on which the delinquent taxpayer took possession of the lands to the (current) date on which the reduced rate was revealed (to be inappropriate). Let this be a warning to other persons. More than this need not be ordered.

Notes

1 The inclusion of this specimen order in this collection reflects the continuing concern of the Mughal imperial administration for keeping all the arable lands of the empire in cultivation. The administration classified as "waste" land (*banjar* or *chachar*), no longer yielding tax revenues, any villages or land left depopulated and uncultivated, whether by natural or man-made disasters, for more than a year or so. Imperial officers usually responded to this problem by reducing revenue demands and/or offering agricultural loans for entrepreneurs who would invest their energy and resources in restoring those waste areas to cultivation. Often such men attracted to the areas given them colonists of migrants from neighboring villages. The reduced assessment for the first three years of renewed cultivation is expressed in terms of the total population. That is, the rate of assessment the first year would be one-fifth of the total harvest, one-fourth the second year and one-third the third year. According to Irfan Habib, the normal practice was to raise this demand to the full one-half for grain crops in the fifth year. Cf. Habib, *The Agrarian System*, pp. 251–253. The proportions given here vary somewhat from those Habib cites for the reduced rate. Also, this document does not state whether the tax demand would be paid in kind or in cash. The mode of assessment was probably crop-sharing rather than a reduction calculated from the rate set out in the previous crop-rate schedules, outdated by the interruption of cultivation.

239a Regulation Exempting Irrigated Lands (*Bāgh*) from Taxation

They (officials) are not to disturb (the cultivators) for the purpose of revenue collection, if income (on that irrigated land) is equal to expenditure (for water), or income is less than expenditure. However, if income is greater than expenditure, they may demand one-sixth portion (of the total produce) from Muslims and one-fourth portion from Hindus. Therefore let them carry out their work in conformity with the regulation of the *ṣadr.*[1]

Notes

1 This possessive construction is not entirely clear. Possibly the regulation in question set up differential sectarian treatment in this area, which was administered by the imperial *ṣadr*, the chief religious officer for Muslim institutions and offices. Although the text is generally free from copyist's errors, this word may also have been an error for *ṣudūr* (issued, emanated).

239a Transmittal Officer (in charge of) Despatching Money and Account Papers of the Subdistrict

This order is issued to that intrepid one ______: the position of transmittal officer (*sazāwal*) officially responsible for the funds of the sublime state and for the despatch of the account papers of ______ subdistrict, ______ district and ______ province has been conferred upon
239b (him) by his solemn agreement. Therefore, he must fulfill the duties and customary obligations of this position. He must not permit the slightest matter to escape his vigilance and care. In cooperation with the *amīn* of that place, and with extreme care, he must send the accumulated revenue collections of those *maḥals*, by means of reliable merchants' bills (*hunḍūyāt*), to his Resplendent Majesty. He must also send to His Resplendent Majesty the papers for the assessment roll,[1] for receipts and arrears, etc. He must prevent any delay or procrastination in the transmittal of the papers and the money. He is to know that there are strict injunctions in this matter.

Notes

1 The *daul-jamaᶜ* listed the *jāgīrdārs'* holdings within a subdistrict or larger unit, along with the valuation assessed for each assignment.

239b Order for Monthly Salary Payment Allocated from the General Treasury

This order is issued to Sanbhunath, treasurer of the general treasury of the Stirrup of Felicity (the camp of the Emperor): in accordance with the exalted command, the sum of five hundred rupees per month is to be paid from the (funds in his) charge to the most worthy ______. (This payment) to assist with living expenses is to be made from the beginning of ______. He may pay the monthly allowance of that aforesaid *khān* in each month from the beginning of (the month) mentioned above. After taking a receipt as established by practice, he will pay the monthly salary to other stipendiaries of that place. Henceforth, in conformity with (the conditions) of this order and receipt, he will set aside and compute (that allowance) for his (the recipient's) account.

239b **Order for Payment to the Animal Stables (*Kārkhāna-i Dawābb*)**

This order is issued to ______, treasurer: he is to pay ten thousand rupees from the funds in his charge from the beginning of ______ as allowance for the feed, etc., of the horse stables, the elephant stables, or other stables for beasts in the charge of ______, the cashkeeper. Having removed the aforesaid sum from his own control and placed it in the control of the cashkeeper, ______, he must obtain a receipt bearing the seals of the officers of that aforementioned establishment. Hereafter he will make allowances for and calculate (that amount) from his accounts in
240a accordance with this present order and receipt.

240a **Order for Payment of Monthly Salary to a *Manṣabdār* from the *Maḥals* of *Sā'ir***

This order is issued to the officers of the cloth market or the Royal Market, or other *maḥals* of *sā'ir*: the sum of ______ (amount) rupees per month is to be paid from the revenues of that place to ______, *manṣabdār*, of ______ *firqat* (company) attached to the *makān* (establishment) of ______. It is decreed that they may pay the allowance of the aforementioned person commencing from ______ (date), as previously established by regulation and custom for the regular stipendiaries of that place. And they must ensure that a receipt is given to the treasurer of that place. Henceforth, in accordance with this order and receipt, (this sum) will be set aside and calculated for their account.

فهرست شرح اسناد خدمات اهلیجات ارباب طلب جمله شصت و پنج سند

صوبه‌داری بموجب فرمان والاشان	نیابت صوبه‌داری	دیوانی صوبه	فوجداری و امانت محالات
فوجداری جاگیر	کروری محالات	فوطه‌داری پرگنه	چودهرائی قانونگوی
زمینداری	برآمدنویسی پرگنه	پروانه بیاض امانت و فوجداری	داروغگی خزانه پرگنه
تحویلداری محال سایر	مشرفی محال سایر	پیشکاری امانت و فوجداری پرگنه	داروغگی و امینی دارالضرب
صاحب عیاری دارالضرب	چودهرائی محال سایر	کوتوالی سکات ولده	مقیمی و مهرداری
داروغگی جوی آب	داروغگی ڈاکچوکی	داروغگی و امینی محال زعفران	داروغگی و امینی پنبه نخاس
پیمانه‌کشی	محلکا خدمت امانت و فوجداری	قبولیت تعهد خدمت امانت و فوجداری	متصدیگری سورت بندر مبارک
دیوانی فوج	امانت پایباقی	کروری محال پایباقی و بازیافت [illegible]	خدمت رفع ابواب ممنوعه
سپردن داغهای طلب منصب خاص	راهداری و نهانه‌داری	خدمت ارزانی تومان پشاور	داروغگی کچهری

داروغگی مبیع غلات	خدمت استیفاء	پیشکاری دیوانی فوج	داروغگی و امینی سایر
دستک و سنجانه برای گزیدن جانوران	جوکسای و وزن‌کشی دارالضرب	قبض نویسی منصبداران	امینی تنخواه دستی روزینه‌داران و غیره
میربندری فرضه و داروغگی تمکابندر	میربحری و داروغگی نواره	امینی کوتوالی	پیشکاری دیوان منصوبه
داروغگی و ناظری جهازات	داروغگی خزانه صوبه یا پرگنه	چودهرائی صرافه	مشرفی پرگنه
کرورائی خزانه و نزاولی دریا طرف پرگنه	اخبارنویسی پرگنه	داروغگی خزانه و نزاولی کاغذ صوبه	مشرفی بندخانه
مردهائی باذیه‌گری با نظارت سادات	حسب الحکم بنام ناظم صوبه بحال تنخواه دستگردان ساهوان	پروانه بنام دیوان صوبه بحال تنخواه مدیر	پروانه کاشت زمین بضابطه کم دستور
پروانه ضابطه معافی محصول ساع	نزاولی ارسال کاغذ پرگنه	دستک تنخواه ساهم مدد خرج از خزانه	دستک تنخواه کارخانجات و دواب سرکار
دستک تنخواه در دامه منصبداران از محال سایر			

شرح اسناد خدمات موافق دفتر والا

خدمت صوبه داری بموجب فرمان والاشان مقرر شود و سند نیابت آن
از دفتر والا در خالصه شریفه قلمی آید حسب الحکم اعلی خدمت نیابت صوبه داری صوبه فلان
که اصالتاً به امارت مرتبت فلان مقرر شده بشهامت و عوالی منزلت فلان تفویض یافته
باید که در نظم و نسق و تمشیت مهمات آن صوبه و محافظت و محارست بلاد و امصار و تنبیه و
تادیب مفسدان و گردنکشان و قلع و قمع بنیه فتنه انگیزان و امنیت طرق و شوارع و امداد
و اعانت فوجداران و امنای محال خالصه شریفه و پایباقی و کماشتهای جاگیرداران
و عدم اخذ ابواب ممنوعه بارگاه معلی و رفع و دفع مهمات و مسکرات سعی و اهتمام
بلیغ بجا آورد و تقید تمام بکار برد که احدی از قوی دست تعدی بحال ضعفا و از
نتواند کرد باید که متصدیان مهمات و عمال و فوجداران خان مشارالیه را نایب ناظم
آن صوبه دانسته دست تصرف او را در اجرای امور مصالحه آن قدر می شناسند
و از سخن و صلاح و صواب دید جناب خان مومی الیه بیرون نروند و خدمت دیوانی صوبه
حسب الحکم اعلی خدمت دیوانی صوبه فلان از تغیر فلان بفلان از ابتدای فصل

215b

حسب الضمن مقرر و مفوض گشته که بلوازم و مراسم خدمت مذکور باید که
در راستی بپردازد و در پرداخت محال خالصه شریفه آن صوبه و تسلی و استمالت
رعایا و ازدیاد و آبادانی و افزونی معموری و تکثیر زراعت دقیقه از دقایق
نامرعی نگذارد و آنچنان نماید که تعدی از عمال در اخذ خراج زیاده از نصف
باندازه و طریقه که در شرع انور و ملت خلیفه اطهر مقرر گشته از رعایا طلب نکند
تا نقصانی و ضرری برعایا نرسد و گنجایش در تعلقات زمینداران متغلب
نگذارد و از عمال و کروریان و فوطه داران خبردار بوده دست تغلب و تصرف
آنها کوتاه دارد و قدغن نماید که هیچیکی از عمال الصوبه نهب و بالادستی در تحصیل ای
و تیه داری و خرج صادر و وارد و دیگر ابواب که بمقتضای رعیت پروری از
پیشگاه کرم گستری معاف شده از رعایا طلب ننماید و اگر شخصی از عمال دست
تصرف بابواب علیه و وجوه محفوه دراز کند باستی در تحصیل نماید حقیقت او را
از روی نفس الامر در حق نوعی که اگر بالحال تفتیش آن بمیان آید خلاف
ظاهر نشود و محول باغراض نفسانی که در کار باد موم است نکرده و نمود

216a

که مطابق آن بعرض اشرف اقدس رسید و بجای او دیگری از حضور معین گردد و اصلا
بی حکم والا اجرات تغیر و تبدیل نکند و هر عاملی که معزول شود بازیافت و بازخواستی که از
باید کرد روبرو کرده بحضور بفرستد که آمده محاسبه بگذراند و از راه احتیاط در
هر فصل از هر پرگنه کاغذ چند دیه گرفته ترجمان فارسی کنند اگر از روی آن ظاهر شود که عمال
زری از ابواب ممنوعه و وجوه طلبه متصرف شده اند روبرو از آنها بازخواست کنند و
ترجمان الخصوص رسالدار دکه درخور کردار بسزا رسیده در حبس مقید باشند تا متعلقان
دیگر عبرت گیرند و در صورت عدم ظهور تصرف عامل را اگر حکم خدمت دارد دستخط دیوانی و
طوامیر و دیگر کاغذ را فصل بفصل سال بسال بقاعده معینه بدفترخانه معلی رسانیده باشد
و از چودهریان و قانونگویان مچلکا بگیرد که بر تقدیر تصرف عاملان در ابواب مرفوعه حقیقت
حال ظاهر نمایند و اگر در اظهار آن مداهنه و مساهله ورزند عرضداشت نماید که آنها از خدمات
معزول گردیده از موطن و مسکن اخراج یابند و مقرر سازد که منجمله بقایا و تقاوی که از
سنه جلوس و در عهد حضرت خلد مکان نزد رعایا طلب باشد از مواضع با قید ... حال
که امتناع تشخیص آن نموده باشند مبلغ پنج روپیه بری یکصد روپیه در هر فصل محال ...

بوصول رساند و زری که بصیغه تقاوی در سالگذشته از سرکار والا تنخواه شده باشد آنرا
با باقی سالها بور در اول توزیع محصول سالحال بگیرد و از وجه حق التحصیل کروریان مکرر ...
بر متصدیان عوض برآمد موقوف داشته تتمه را منجمله بقایا بموجب اسناد علحده ...
باشد و اگر احیاناً وجه مذکوره بتنخواه حق التحصیل وفا نکند قدر زاید را از محصول سالحال
تنخواه نماید باید که متصدیان مهمات انجا مومی الیه را دیوان مستقل دانسته لوازم و
لواحق آن بمشار الیه متعلق شناسند و دست احدی ورا در اجرای امور مضافه
و متعلقه آن قوی دانند و در جناب تأکید دانند خدمت فوجداری و امانت در مولای حسب الحکم الاعلی
خدمت فوجداری و امانت پرگنه فلان سرکار فلان صوبه فلان از تغیر فلان بفلان من ابتدا
فصل فلان حسب الضمن مقرر و مفوض گشته که بلوازم و مراسم آن بخدمت از قرار واقع
دقیقه از دقایق حزم و احتیاط فروگذار ندارد و در ضبط و ربط و تنبیه و تادیب مفسدان
و سرکشان ... قلاع آنها تفریق و حفظ و حراست رهروان و رهگذاران و منع اندازان
... مساعی جمیله بکار برد و به بهانه داران که بواسطه ضبط و ربط تعین کنند
قدغن نماید که چیزی بصیغه ابواب ممنوعه نگیرند و از مفسدان و ... از دیهات آن محال ...

فساد باشند و عامل در باره تنبیه آنها نوشته بدهد اول احدی را از آنها
بدست آورده در اصلاح بکوشد که از تمرد و سرتابی نادم شده بمالگذاری و زراعتی تن
در دهند و بر تقدیر اصلاح رضانامه از عامل بگیرد و اگر از شقاوت جبلی باصلاح نیایند
بموجب حکم تاخته تنبیه مفسدان نماید و رعایای ریزه را ایذا نرساند و غنیمتی که از مواشی
وغیره بدست آید از عامل تسلیم نموده قبض بگیرد یا عوض مال واجب موضع بور در
سرکار ضبط نماید و بندی نکند مگر در دار الحرب و محافظت طرق و شوارع نوعی نماید
که مسافرین و متردّدین بجمعیت خاطر و طمانیت باطن آمد و شد نموده باشند و در
هیچ جا دزدی و رهزنی بوقوع نیاید و اگر احیاناً مال کسی بدزدی و یا بغارت رود
آنرا با دزدان و رهزنان پیدا ساخته مال را بمالک و انجامع بدمال را بسزا رساند و در
صورت پیدا نساختن از عهده جواب مال مذبور برآید و احتیاط نماید که منهیات و مسکرات
در آنمحال بعمل در نیاید و در تسلی و استمالت رعایا و افزونی زراعت هر موضع سعی بلیغ نماید
و بهر ربیع و خریف مطلع شده جمع و اخراجات هر سال از روی خسره بعد ملاحظه بعمل آرد
بدیهی دریافت احوال رعایا بنوعی که بر ریزه رعایا سختی نرود و گنجایش در تحصیل

نماند و نصف سالم برعایا و نصف بی نقصان بسرکار والا رسد تشخیص نموده بکروری
تاکید کند که بتحصیل درآورده تحویل فوطه دار نماید و زر یکه از سنه چهل و دو عهد حضرت جلالی مکانی
نزد رعایا باقی باشد بکروری قدغن نماید که بر تصدیق بجز و بمرجع حال که تشخیص درآید در هر فصل
تا وصول آن بتحصیل درآورد و آنچه بصیغه تقاوی در سالگذشته برعایا تنخواه شده باشد
آنرا با باقی سالهای پیش در اول توزیع سال حال بگیرد که در صورت اهمال باز خواست از و
خواهد شد و احتیاط بکار برد که کروری جرات باخذ ابواب و وجوه ممنوعه بارگاه والا نکند
و محافظت زر تحویل فوطه دار و باز خواست مبلغی که از عین المال یا برداشت کند زر
او باقی ماند مطابق دستور مقرر بعهده خود شناسد و باخبر باشد که فوطه دار یکدام
بی سند معتبر دیوان پسند خرج نکند و زر مسطور را بخزانه عامره رسانیده قبض الوصول
آن به فوطه دار بدهد و بر طبق قاعده معین از وجه حق التحصیل کروری بگیرد و عوض برآید
موقوف داشته داخل در جمع نماید که تا فی الحال در برآمد کروری مجرا خواهد شد و باقی را
بموجب سند حضور منجمله زر تقاوی و تقاوی که بوصول رسد بتصدیق خود کروری تنخواه
میداده باشد و بر تقدیریکه زر مسطور تنخواه حق التحصیل وفا نکند قدر زاید را از تحصیل

سالحال تن نماید و دوجمع و دیگر سررشته کاغذ هر فصل را درست کرده بحضور پر نور
میفرستاده باشد باید که چودهریان و قانونگویان و مقدمان و رعایا و مزارعان آنجا
مومی الیه را فوجدار و امین آنمحال دانسته از سخن صلاح و صوابدید شان که هرآینه متضمن بهبود دولت
در انجام معاملات و کفایت سرکار والا و رفاهیت رعایا و مالگذار و تقاوی آبادی بود باشند
[illegible] لوازم و لواحق آن خدمت با متعلق شناسند فوجداری جاگیر در نولا
حسب الحکم اعلی خدمت فوجداری و اهمام جاگیر فلان که در پرگنه فلان سرکار و صوبه فلان
تنخواه است حسب الضمن از تغیر فلان بعهده فلان مقرر شده باید که بلوازم و مراسم آن از
قرار واقع پرداخته در ضبط و ربط و تنبیه و تادیب مفسدان و متمردان و هدم قلاع آن فرقه
و حفظ و حراست زیردستان و مالگذاران و منع آهنگران از ساختن بندوق کوشش واقعی
کوشد و جمعی که به تهانجات محال فوجداری بواسطه بند و بست و ضبط و ربط تعین کند
تاکید نماید که چیزی بصیغه ابواب ممنوعه نگیرند و احدی مرتکب منهیات و مسکرات نگردد
و اگر مفسدان در دیهی از دیهات آنمحال مصدر فساد باشند اولا چندی برای آنجا عهد دست
آورده در صلاح بکوشد که از تمرد و سرتابی نادم شده بمالگذاری و رعیتی تن در دهد

و اگر از شقاوت جبلی با صلاح نیایند بر آن موضع تاخته مفسدان نماید و در زمره رعایا را
آزار نرساند و بندی نکند مگر در دار الحرب و محافظت شاهراه نوعی نماید که مسافرین
و متردین بجمعیت خاطر و طمانیت باطن آمد و شد نموده باشند و در هیچ جا دزدی
و رهزنی بوقوع نیاید و اگر احیاناً مال کسی بدزدی یا بغارت رود دزدان و رهزنان را
پیدا ساخته مال را بمالک و آنچه عهد مال را بسرکار رساند و در صورت پیدا ساختن از
عهده جواب مال بدر برآید باید که چودهریان و قانونگویان و رعایا و مقدمان و مزارعان
آنجا مومی الیه را فوجدار محال جاگیر مسطور دانسته لوازم و لواحق آن خدمت با متعلق دانند
و در هیچ باب تاکید شناسند خدمت کروری در نولا حسب الحکم اعلی خدمت کروری
پرگنه فلان سرکار و صوبه فلان از تغیر فلان مطابق ضمن از ابتدای فلان بفلان مقرر شده
باید که بلوازم و مراسم آن براستی و درستی پرداخته در ازدیاد آبادانی و افزونی و معموری
و کثرت زراعت و فراهم آوردن رعایا بواقعی کوشد و محصول و حقوق دیوانی آنمحال را مطابق
تشخیص امین باوام آخر بوصول آورده بتحویل فوطه دار نماید و یکدام علیحده نگاه ندارد
و از احد ابواب طلبه و وجوه ممنوعه محترز و مجتنب باشد و منجمله حق التحصیل خود بطور عوض

برآمد ابواب جمع نماید و تتمه را منجمله زریکه از بقایا و تقاوی بوصول رسد بتصدیق
امین بگیرد و زریکه از بقایا و تقاوی سنوات که از سنه چهل و دو عهد حضرت جنت مکان
نزد رعایا باقی باشد از مواضع با قید ز جمع حال که امین تشخیص نماید بتجربه بر تصدیق بمال در
هر فصل باتفاق امین بوصول رساند و زریکه بصیغه تقاوی در سال گذشته از سرکار ادا
برعایا تنخواه شده باشد در اول توزیع محصول سال حال بگیرد و بر نقد را اهمال با اجرا
آن بعهده خود شناسد و هر قدر زر رعایا به فوطه خانه بیارد جهتی آن بمهر خود
و دستخط فوطه دار با آنها بدهاند و هنگام میاقی و اصلات را موافق
همان جهتی ها محسوب گرداند و سوای زر واجب چیزی بصیغه بهنت و تحصیلداری
و دیگر ابواب طلب نگیرد و مجمل و جمع خرج و دیگر سر رشته کاغذ را موافق ضابطه
معمول به فرخانه معلی میرسانیده باشد. باید که چودهریان و قانونگویان و مقدمان و
رعایا و مزارعان آنمحال مشار الیه را کروری آنجا دانسته لوازم و لواحق آنخدمت
باو متعلق دانند خدمت فوطه داری در نیولا خدمت فوطه داری پرگنه فلان سرکار فلان
از تغیر فلان مطابق ضمن ابتدای فلان بفلان مقرر شده که بلوازم و مراسم آنخدمت

براستی و درستی پرداخته دقیقه از دقایق حزم و هوشیاری و احتیاط
غیر مرعی نگذارد و زریکه از محصول آنجا فراهم آید با احتیاط تمام در حجره
فوطه خود نگاه داشته و در آن را بمهر خود و امین مقفل داشته باتفاق
یکدیگر بگشاید و بربندد و یکدام بی سند معتبر دیوان بسند بخرج نیارد
و تمامی زر تحویل خود را باستصواب امین خزانه عامره رسانیده قبض الوصول
بگیرد باید که متصدیان مهمات آنجا مومی الیه را فوطه دار آنمحال دانسته
لوازم و لواحق آنخدمت باو متعلق شناسند و هرچه بتحصیل درآید رو برو
تحویل او نموده چیزی علحده نگاه ندارند و درینباب تاکید دانند خدمت چودهرائی
و قانونگوئی متصدیان مهمات و متکفلان معاملات حال و استقبال بدانند
که درینولا حسب الحکم اعلی خدمت چودهرائی قانونگوئی پرگنه فلان از تغیر فلان
بقبول مبلغ انیقدر پیشکش سرکار معلی مطابق ضمن مقرر و مفوض شده که بلوازم
و مراسم آنخدمت قیام نموده در دلنخواهی و کفایت سرکار والا و آبادی
و استمالت رعایا و افزونی زراعت مساعی جمیله بظهور رسانیده دقیقه از

دقایق حزم و هوشیاری نامرعی نگذارد و موازنه و دستور العمل و دیگر
سررشته کاغذ حالی اصل و جمعدامی وغیره موافق ضابطه و معمول سال بسال
معرفت دیوان صوبه بدفترخانه والا میرسانیده باشد و بدعت احداث
ننماید و رعایا و برایا و دیگر سکنه آنجا را بحسن سلوک راضی داشته
بر امور تغلب و تعدی نکرده و چیزی از کسی سوای رسوم مقرری که قطع و توقع
ننماید باید که چودهریان و قانونگویان و مقدمان و رعایا مشارالیه را قانونگوی
آنجا دانسته از سخن حسابی و صلاح صوابدید او که هرآینه متضمن کفایت سرکار والا
و رفاهیت رعایا و مالگذار باشد بیرون نروند در عیناب تاکید دانند زمینداری
متصدیان مهمات و متکفلان معاملات و چودهریان و قانونگویان و مقدمان
پرگنه فلان سرکار صوبه فلان بدانند که درینولا حسب الحکم اعلی خدمت زمینداری
محال مسطور مطابق ضمن از تغیر فلان بقبول مبلغ اینقدر [illegible] متکفلی سرکار معلی
بفلان مقرر شده که بلوازم و مراسم آن از روا [illegible] تا کاذ رعایا و
برایا سلوک پسندیده نماید و در اخراج و تنبیه و تادیب مفسدان [illegible]

موفور بظهور رساند و چنان کند که اثری از دزدان و رهزنان در آن سرزمین ساعی
نماند و در تسلی و استمالت رعایا و افزونی زراعت و ازدیاد آبادی و اظهار
مراسم دولتخواهی کوشش فراوان بکار برد و نوعی بندوبست نماید که مفسدان
مخرج را اصلا مجال مداخلت در آن محال نباشد و از شاهراه نوعی خبردار باشد که
مسافرین و متردین بجمعیت خاطر و طمانیت باطن آمد و شد مینموده باشند و در
هیچ جا دزدی و رهزنی بوقوع نیاید و اگر مال کسی بدزدی یا بغارت رود
دزدان و رهزنان را پیدا ساخته مال را بمالک و آنجا عه بد مال را بسزا رساند و در صورت
پیدا نساختن از عهده جواب بالمذبور برآید و تقید نماید که احدی در حدود متعلقه
زمینداری او مرتکب منهیات و مسکرات نگردد و باید که مشارالیه را زمیندار محال
مرقوم دانسته لوازم و لواحق این خدمت با و متعلق دانند خدمت برآمد نویسی
متصدیان مهمات سرکار و صوبه فلان بدانند که درینولا حسب الحکم اعلی خدمت
برآمد نویسی محال معروض آنجا از تغیر فلان بفلان مطابق ضمن مقرر شده که بلوازم
و مراسم آن خدمت بدیانت و راستی قیام نموده دقیقه از دقایق حزم

و احتیاط غیر مرعی نگذارد و برآمد عمال معزول از روی کاغذ خام اصلی که مبرا
از شایبه تلبیس باشد بدقت تمام بنحوی که حرفی پوشیده و پنهان نماند و
بر احدی از عاملان حیف و میل نرود و بمواجهه گماشته عمال باتفاق داروغه
تحقیق آورده طوامیر آن را بضابطه مقرر درست ساخته بتصدیق داروغه
و خود و بدستخط چودهریان و قانونگویان بدفتر معلی رساند تا بموجب آن
بازخواستی و بازیافتی که از هر کدام باید نمود بعمل درآید باید که اینها مشار الیه را
برآمدنویس آن محال دانسته لوازم و لواحق این خدمت را متعلق باو دانند
و در احضار و ارجاع چودهریان و قانونگویان و مقدمان و دیگر عمله و فعله و در رسانیدن
کاغذی که جهت تفتیش این معامله درکار باشد توقف نکنند و رفاقت و همراهی مشار الیه
در انجام این کار بوجه احسن نمایند پروانه بیاضی امانت و فوجداری رعیت و ...
امانت دستگاه محفوظ باشند درین ولا حسب الحکم اشرف اقدس اعلی خدمت
امانت و فوجداری پرگنه فلان سرکار و صوبه فلان من ابتدای فلان بتغیر فلان بفلان
مقرر و مفوض شده باید که شکرانه این موهبت عظمی بجا آورده دقیقه‌ای از ...

سربابان و حفظ و حراست زیردستان و مالگذاران و گردآوری مال واجب
سرکار معلی و افزونی زراعت و کثرت معموری مساعی جمیله بکار برد و مال واجب را
بروقت و هنگام بمعرض تشخیص و تحصیل درآورده بر سبیل هندویات صرافان
معتبر بحضور پرنور رسانیده باشد متعاقب وکیل آن رفعت پناه سند ضمنی حاصل
کرده خواهد فرستاد خدمت داروغگی خزانه پرگنه دستک باسم متصدیان مهمات
خزانه پرگنه فلان سرکار و صوبه فلان آنکه درینولا حسب الحکم اعلی داروغگی خزانه مذکور از
تغیر فلان بفلان مقرر شده که بلوازم و مراسم این خدمت بدیانت و امانت پرداخته دقیقه
از دقایق حزم و هوشیاری غیر مرعی نگذارد و محافظت خزانه در واقعی نماید و هر که را
آید در خزانه نگاه داشته در آن را بمهر خود و خزانچی مقفل داشته بحضور خود بگشاید و بندد و
و زر را بقاعده معین مقرر باحتیاط تمام مصحوب جمعیت فوجدار بخزانه عامره صوبه رسانیده
باشند و قبض بخط خزانچی باشد و تقید بکار برد که دام و درم بی سند معتبر دیوانی صرف نشود
و احدی دست تصرف دراز نتواند کرد باید که مشار الیه داروغه خزانه مذکور
دانسته لوازم و لواحق این خدمت را متعلق او دانند خدمت تحویلداری دستک محال سرکار

باسم متصدیان مهمات محال سایر فلان صوبه فلان آنکه در ینولا خدمت
تحویلداری محال مذبور از تغیر فلان بفلان مقرر شده که بلوازم و مراسم آنخدمت
بدیانت و راستی تمام پرداخته دقیقه از دقایق حزم و احتیاط نامرعی
نگذارد و زریکه تحویل او شود با احتیاط تمام در کوتهه زیر مهر خود و داروغه
نگاهداشته دامی بدون سند معتبر دیوان سند خرج نکند و تمامی زر تحویل خود
باستصواب امین بخزانه عامره رسانیده قبض الوصول بگیرد باید که موجب ...
تحویلدار آنمحال دانسته لوازم و لواحق آنخدمت با و متعلق دانند و آنچه از محصول آنمحال
بوصول درآید تحویل او نموده چیزی علحده نگاهدارند خدمت مشرفی محال سایر
دستک باسم متصدیان مهمات مال سایر فلان متعلقه صوبه فلان آنکه در ینولا
خدمت مشرفی آنجا از تغیر فلان بفلان مقرر شده که بلوازم و مراسم آنخدمت
براستی و درستی پرداخته دقیقه از دقایق حزم و احتیاط نامرعی نگذارد و کاغذ
موافق ضابطه مقرر و قاعده معین درست ساخته بدفترخانه عالی رسانیده باشد
باید که آنها او را مشرف آنجا دانسته لوازم و لواحق آنخدمت با و متعلق [illegible]

خدمت بیتکاری فوجداری [illegible] دستک باسم زبدة الاماثل والاقران آنکه در ینولا خدمت
بیتکاری فوجدار و امین محال فلان از تغیر فلان مقرر شده باید که بلوازم و
مراسم آن بدیانت و راستی از قرار واقع پرداخته دقیقه از دقایق حزم
و هوشیاری غیر مرعی نگذارد و در جمیع معاملات آنجا نوعی خبرداری
بکار برد که فوت و فروگذاشت دامی بوقوع نیاید و سررشته کاغذ را موافق
ضابطه بر طبق قاعده معین و مقرر مفصل و منقح درست کرده بدفترخانه معلی رسانیده
باشد در ینباب تاکید دانند خدمت داروغگی دار الضرب دستک باسم
متصدیان مهمات و عمله و فعله دار الضرب واقعه صوبه فلان آنکه در ینولا حسب الحکم
خدمت داروغگی محال مذبور از تغیر فلان بفلان مقرر شده که بلوازم و مراسم آنخدمت
بدیانت و راستی پرداخته دقیقه از دقایق حزم و احتیاط نامرعی نگذارد و
و تقید بکار برد که محصول آنمحال بضابطه مقرر و قاعده معین منضبط درآید و فوت و
فروگذاشت نشود و اشرفی و روپیه وغیره خوشخط و بوزن و عیار کامل بسکه مبارک
مسکوک میشده باشد و محافظت و نگهبانی زر تحویل خزانچی بعهده خود دانسته

نگذارد که دامی بدون سند معتبر دیوان سند بخرج تواند رفت باید که آنها بمومی الیه
را امین آنمحال دانسته لوازم و لواحق آنخدمت با و متعلق دانند زیاده باکلید
خدمت صاحب عیاری دار الضرب دستک باسم متصدیان مهمات و عمله و فعله دار الضرب
واقعه صوبه فلان آنکه درینولا خدمت صاحب عیاری محال مذبور از تغیر فلان بفلان
مقرر شده باید که بلوازم و مراسم آنخدمت قرار واقع از راستی و درستی و
دقیقه از دقایق حزم و هوشیاری نامرعی نگذارد و اشرفی و روپیه وغیره بعیار کامل
موافق ضابطه مقرر بسکه مبارک رساند باید که آنها مشار الیه را صاحب عیار
آنجا دانسته لوازم و لواحق آنخدمت با و متعلق شناسند خدمت چودهرائی
محال سایر دستک باسم متصدیان مهمات و عمله و فعله محال سایر پرگنه فلان
صوبه فلان آنکه درینولا خدمت چودهرائی محال مذبور بقبول پیشکش انقدر روپیه
سرکار والا از تغیر فلان بفلان مقرر گشته که بلوازم و مراسم آنخدمت قرار واقع
پرداخته دقیقه از دقایق حزم و احتیاط غیر مرعی نگذارد و بیوپاریان از حسن سلوک
خود راضی داشته پیرامون تغلب نگردد و در دولتخواهی و کردآوری محصول

سرکار والا آنچه لازمه تقید است بتقدیم رساند باید که آنها خدمت مذبور را
بمشار الیه مقرر و مفوض دانسته لوازم و لواحق آنخدمت با و متعلق شناسند و
در مهمات تاکید دانند خدمت کوتوالی کابلبند دستک باسم متصدیان مهمات
و عمله و فعله چبوتره کوتوالی دار السعادت یا بلده فلان صوبه فلان آنکه درینولا
حسب الحکم اعلی خدمت کوتوالی بلده مذبور از تغیر فلان بفلان مقرر شده که لوازم
و مراسم آنخدمت از راستی و درستی پرداخته دقیقه از دقایق حزم و
هوشیاری غیر مرعی نگذارد و از احوال سکنه آنجا بواقعی خبردار بوده در ضبط و
ربط و محافظت شهر و پاسبانی شب سعی فراوان بکار برد و نوعی بندوبست نماید
که دزدی نشود و در صورت وقوع دزدی سارقان را با مال پیدا ساخته مال را
بمالک و دزدان بسزا رساند و الا از عهده آن جواب گوید و تقید بکار برد که
احدی مرتکب جور و تعدی نشود و مسکرات و منهیات بعمل نیاید و جمعی که بعلت جنایت
گرفتار آیند در باده حبس و خلاص آنها بنحویکه قاضی آنجا برفق و حقیقت آنجا
دستخط کند بعمل آرد و دیگر شهر و عمله و فعله چبوتره کوتوالی سلوک پسندیده نماید

باید که آنها مشار الیه را کوتوال آنجا دانسته لوازم و لواحق آن خدمت را متعلق
شناسند درین باب تاکید دانند خدمت معینی و مهم راهی در ینولا خدمت
مقومی فلان محال از تغیر فلان بفلان مقرر شده که بلوازم و مراسم آن خدمت از
راستی و درستی بپردازد و متاعی که بیوپاریان آن محال بیارند قیمت آن را چنان
مشخص نماید که مابین الحال در آن تفاوت ظاهر نشود و متصدیان آنجا موافق قیمت مذکور
در سرکار والا محصول آن بضبط در آرند سوای دستور مقرری از بیوپاریان
چیزی نگیرد و بیوپاریان از حسن سلوک راضی داشته برامون تغلب نگردد
و در خرید و فروخت چنان تقید بکار برد که نقصان بمال سرکار والا نرسد باید که
آنها او را مقوم آنجا دانسته لوازم و لواحق آن خدمت را متعلق دانند درین باب تاکید دانند
خدمت داروغگی جوی آب دستک باسم متصدیان مهمات و عمله و فعله جوی آب
واقعه فلان آنجا آنکه حسب الحکم اعلی خدمت داروغگی جوی مذبور از تغیر فلان بفلان
مقرر شده که بلوازم و مراسم آن خدمت بدیانت و راستی پرداخته تنخواه آن ما
کشتکار جوی مذبور را بامداد رعایای دهاتی که از جوی مسطور زراعت مینمایند

داروغه

قرار واقع موافق معمول مرمت نماید که آب وافر جاری شود و حصه رسد موافق زراعت
هرکدام دهات متعلقه قسمت کرده بدهد که آبادانی وافزونی محصول آن محال شود و
دولتخواهی سرکار و رفاهیت رعایا بوقوع آید باید که آنها مشار الیه را داروغه
آنجا دانسته لوازم و لواحق آن خدمت را متعلق دانند خدمت داروغگی داک چوکی
دستک باسم فلان آنکه درینولا بر طبق حکم جهان مطاع آفتاب شعاع خدمت
داروغگی داک چوکی صوبه فلان از تغیر فلان با رفعت پناه مقرر و مفوض گشته باید که بلوازم
و مراسم خدمت مأموره قرار واقع پرداخته بنحوی شرایط سعی و اهتمام بجا آرد
که در رسیدن خلوه جات و غیره احکام پادشاهی توقف و تاخیر بوقوع نیاید و فرامین
سعادت آیین و احکام قدسی که متصدیان آنجا شرف صدور یابد باحتیاط رسانیده
عرضداشت و واقعه را مطابق دستور و معمول روانه حضور پر نور نموده باشد و از
هیچ راه محلکا بگیرد که سوای خلوه احکام نوشته غیری را همراه خلوه بحضور بیارند و از
ارتکاب این عمل که از ابواب ممنوعه بارگاه والاست حذر بوده توجهی من آن جوه
مراسم و متعرض احوال مسافرین و مترددین نشوند در سرشته قضایای دارالعدالت

وصورت انفصال معاملات و عدم انفصال آن بقید تفصیل معه کیفیت
و کمیت محبوسان قلعجات و کچهری و سبب قید آنهارا با سوانح رو داد و
شرح آنجا از روی نفس الامر و راستی بی کم و زیاد مفصل نوشته بلا توقف
و اهمال ارسال حضور لامع النور نماید و از رعایت و عداوت محترز باشند زیاده تاکید داند

خدمت دارو غگی و بهمین مضمون امینی محال زعفران دستک باسم متصدیان مهمات
و عمله و فعله محال زعفران پرگنه فلان مضاف صوبه کشمیر آنکه در ینولا خدمت داروغگی
محال مذبور از تغیر فلان بفلان مقرر شده که بلوازم و مراسم آن براستی و درستی
پرداخته دقیقه از دقایق حزم و هوشیاری نامرعی نگذارد و در موسم شگفتن و چیدن
و خشک کردن و تعیین نرخ نظر بر قلت و کثرت زعفران و کفایت سرکار و بشرکت
کار و بیع آن بمشتریان نهایت سعی و تقید بکار برده چنان احتیاط نماید که احدی را
مجال تغلب و تصرف نماند و وجه بهای زعفران بدفتر قرارداد بوصول آورده تقید
بکار برد که اصلا از بقیه بر ذمه خریداران نماند باید که آنها مشار الیه را داروغه
دانسته لوازم و لواحق آن با و متعلق شناسند و در یباب تاکید دانند

خدمت داروغگی و بهمین مضمون امینی مهمات نخاس دستک باسم متصدیان مهمات و
عمله و فعله مهمه نخاس بلده فلان صوبه فلان آنکه در ینولا خدمت داروغگی
آنجا از تغیر فلان بفلان مقرر شده باید که بلوازم و مراسم آنخدمت بدیانت و راستی
پرداخته دقیقه از دقایق حزم و هوشیاری غیر مرعی نگذارد و ضبط حاصلات
بر وفق دستور و ضابطه معین میکرده باشد و نوعی خبردار باشد که در هیچ معامله
فوت و فروگذاشتی بمیان نیاید و احدی را مجال تصرف و تغلب نماند و بوپاریان
هنود جنس خود را داخل امتعه مسلمین نتوانند نمود و محلکاری معنی از دلالان آنجا
بگیرد و محافظت و نگهبانی زر تحویل تحویلدار بعهده خود شناسد و نگذارد که تحویلدار
دامی بدون سند معتبر دیوان بسند صرف تواند نمود و تمامی زر تحویل او را بخزانه
عامره رسانیده قبض الوصول تحویلدار بدهاند باید که آنها مشار الیه را داروغه
آنمحال دانسته لوازم و لواحق آنخدمت باو متعلق شناسند

خدمت بیمانه کشتی
دستک باسم متصدیان مهمات محال خالصه شریفه آنکه در ینولا خدمت
بیمانه کشتی آنمحال از تغیر فلان بفلان مقرر شده باید که بلوازم و مراسم آن براستی

و راستی پرداخته دقیقه از دقایق حزم و هوشیاری غیر مرعی نگذارد و سررشته کاغذ موافق ضابطه بر طبق قاعده معین بدفترخانه معلی میرسانیده باشند
باید که آنها مشار الیه را بیمانه کشتی آنمحال دانسته لوازم و لواحق آنخدمت باو متعلق شناسند و در یباب تاکید دانند

مچلکای خدمت امانت و فوجداری کمینه بنده درگاه خلایق پناه ام چون از پیشگاه
خلافت و جهانبانی فوجداری پرگنه فلان مضاف صوبه فلان بعهده بنده درگاه
از تغیر فلان مقرر گشته نوشته میدهم که بلوازم و مراسم آن براستی و درستی
پرداخته دقیقه از دقایق حزم و احتیاط نامرعی نگذارم و در بندوبست محالات
و تنبیه و تادیب مفسدان و سرتابان و هدم قلاع اهل التفریق و حفظ و حراست زیردستان
و منع متمردان از ساختن بندوق بتواقعی کوشش و جهدی که تهانجات محال فوجداری
باز ضبط و ربط تعین نمایم تاکید کنم که چیزی بصیغه ابواب ممنوعه نگیرند و احدی از آن
مرتکب منهیات و منکرات نگردد و اگر مفسدان دیهی از دیهات تمرد و فساد اختیار نماید
اول اجتیدی از انجماعه بدلاسا و تسلی بدست آورده در اصلاح کوشم که اگر از
در تبایی دم شده پا بگذاری و رعیتی تن در دهند و اگر از شقاوت جبلی باصلاح نیایند
تا دفعه تنبیه مفسدان نمایم و محافظت شاهراه بنوعی نمایم که مسافرین ... خاطر
و طمانیت باطن آید و شد نموده باشند و هیچ جا دزدی و رهزنی ... و اگر
کسی رهزنی یا غارت رود مال را با مالک و انجماعه بدمال را بسزا رسانم و در صورت

پیدا نساختن از عهده جواب مال برآیم و در مال خالصه شریفه دست تصرف نکنم
بنا بران این چند کلمه بطریق مچلکا نوشته دادم که ثانی الحال سند باشد قبولیت
تعهد خدمت امانت و فوجداری چون خدمت امانت و فوجداری پرگنه فلان سرکار و صوبه فلان
محال خالصه شریفه من ابتدای فلان بعوض مبلغ اینقدر روپیه سکه مبارک هرسنه
هر ضرب بهیچ جهه بالعهد خام بلاشرکت غیری از مالوجهات و کلجوبات لغایت فلان واجب
یکساله یا دوساله خواه سه ساله برضا و رغبت خود قبول نمودم و اقرار مینمایم که مبلغ مذکور بشرط
بحالی خدمت فصل بفصل بموجب اقساط ذیل در سرکار والا واصل سازم و در جمع بندی
زناکار وغیره ابواب مخارج بدستور جاگیرداری و معمول مجرا گیرم و خدا نخواسته باشد اگر
آفت سماوی یا ارضی رو دهد بروقت بمتصدیان سرکار اطلاع دهم و بموجب تحقیقات امین حضور
مجرا گیرم و اگر ما بین فصل یا غیر آن آید بعد مجرا خرج جمع بندی وغیره از روی واصلات ... سازم
و واصلات ... معزول بالاتفاق یکدیگر از روی تحقیقات امین حضور و دستخط خود بدهم ...
... بتعهد خود از سرکار مجرا ... تا دام آخر داخل نمایم بنا بران این چند کلمه
... نوشته دادم که ثانی الحال سند باشد خریف چهار قسط ربیع چهار قسط

بموجب سیاهه خام و کاغذ تحریر

خدمت متصدیگری بنیچه مبارکه در نیولا حسب الحکم اعلی خدمت متصدیگری بندر مبارک سورت

منضاف قصوبه زین البلاد احمدآباد از تغیر فلان بفلان من ابتدای فلان حسب الضمن مقرر شده

که بلوازم و مراسم آن از قرار واقع پرداخته تنقیح محاسبات و معاملات و بازخواست

مطالبات عمال نموده باشد و اگر عامل محالی خاین و بدعمل ظاهر شود کیفیت را بحضور پرنور معروض دارد

که بجایش دیگری معین گردد و در تنبیه و تادیب مفسدان و ترابان و هدم قلاع آنها بقدر

حفظ و حراست رهگذر دستان و مالگذاران و منع آهنگران از ساختن بندوق مساعی موفوره

بظهور رساند و به تهانه داران که بنابر بندوبست تعین کنند تاکید نماید که چیزی بصیغه ابواب ممنوعه نگیرند

واحدی مرتکب منهیات و مسکرات نگردد و اگر مفسدان دیهی از دیهات مورد فساد باشند

اولا حیندی را از آنها بدست آورده در اصلاح بکوشد که از تمرد و سرتابی نادم و پشیمان شده

بمالگذاری رعیتی تن در دهند و اگر از شقاوت جبلی باصلاح نیایند بر آنها چیره دست ساخته مفسدان را

در بر عایای ریزه از زر رساند و غنیمتی که از مواشی و غیره بدست آید عوض مالواجب موضع منظور دارد

ضبط کند و محافظت طرق و شوارع نوعی نماید که مسافرین و مترددین بجمعیت خاطر و طمانیت

آمد و شد نموده باشند و در هیچ جا دزدی و رهزنی بوقوع نیاید و اگر احیانا مال کسی بدزدی

227b

یا بغارت رود تجسس باز دزدان و رهزنان پیدا ساخته مال را بمالک و آنجماعه

بدمال را بسزا رساند و در صورت پیدا نساختن از عهده جواب مال مذبور برآید

و در ازدیاد و آبادانی و تکثیر زراعت و فراهم آوردن رعایا و تسلی و استمالت

آنها و تشخیص و تحصیل مالواجب محالات خالصه شریفه نوعی که نصف سالم برعایا

و نصف بی نقصان بسرکار والا برسد مساعی موفوره بظهور رساند و به کروریان

قدغن نماید که زر محصول موافق تشخیص بوقت تحصیل نموده تحویل فوطه داران نماید

و تا وصول بقایای سنوات از مواضع باقیدار بجزو به بر تصدیق تحصیل در آورده داخل خزانه

نماید و اجیانا اینکار بر دگر کروریان و فوطه داران دست تصرف بمال سرکار معلی

دراز کنند و محافظت خزانه و بازخواست مبلغی که از عین المال نزد خزانچی و فوطه دار

و تحویلداران باقی باشد بعهده خود دانسته از تحویل آنها بخزانه جمع گردانیده قبض الوصول

بآنها بدهد و از اخراجات حق التحصیل کروریان بکرو به بر تصدیق عوض برآید موقوف داشته

باینها هیچ جهت منکوب بموجب سند حضور پرنور منجمله زر بقایا و تقاوی که بوصول رسد

تحواله نموده باشد و اگر زر مذبور بتنخواه حق التحصیل کفایت نکند قدر زاید را

228a

از محصول سال‌الحال تن نماید و بضبط محصول بنا در قرار واقعی بپردازد و با تاجران سلوک پسندیده نماید و هرگاه فصل بآخر رسد از روی کاغذ تحقیقات تغلب و تصرف عمال نموده هرچه بنام آنها ظاهر شود بازخواست نماید و حراست حصار بندر مبارک سورت بواقعی نماید باید که عمال و چودهریان و قانونگویان و مقدمان و مزارعان و رعایای آنجا مشارالیه را متصدی بندر مسطور دانسته لوازم و لواحق اینخدمت بومی الیه متعلق شناسند و از سخن صلاح و صوابدید حسابی او که هر آینه متضمن نفع سرکار و رفاهیت رعایا باشد بیرون نروند و شکر و شکایات او را درباره خود مؤثر دانند خدمت دیوانی فوج درینولا حسب الحکم اعلی خدمت دیوانی فوج همراهی فلان بفلان مقرر شده که بلوازم و مراسم اینخدمت از دیانت و راستی پرداخته دقیقه از دقایق حزم و هوشیاری مهمل و نامرعی نگذارد و زر که جهت تنخواه سپاه و دیگر ارباب طلب در خزانه فوج فراهم آید مهر و مهر خود امانت داشته طلب طلبداران بعد ملاحظه موجودات بموجب سند حضور پرنور تنخواه دهد و نشود که ازو مبلغی بدون سند معتبر دیوان پسند بخرج درآید والا بازیافت و بازپرس آن خواهد شد

خود داند و نسخه دیوانی و جمع و خرج واصل سه خزانه و دیگر سررشته کاغذ موافق ضابطه و معمول به دفترخانه معلی میرسانیده باشد و با عمله و فعله و ارباب طلب سلوک پسندیده نماید و مرتکب تعدی نشود باید که مشارالیه را دیوان فوج مذکور دانسته لوازم و لواحق اینخدمت با او متعلق شناسند خدمت امانت یا بیاقی درینولا خدمت امانت یا بیاقی واراضی بازیافت ایمه ارباب وظایف و معاش پرگنه فلان صوبه فلان از تغیر فلان بفلان حسب التضمن من ابتدای فلان مقرر شده که بلوازم و مراسم اینخدمت بدیانت و راستی پرداخته با کافه رعایا سلوک پسندیده نماید و محالی که در باب بیاقی درآید از قرار واقع بضبط درآورده تا تنخواه شدن بجاگیرداران جمع آن را بعد ملاحظه جمع سنوات عمل جاگیرداران پیشین و موجودات حال بجز رسی تمام بنحوی که نصف برعایا و نصف به سرکار والا برسد مشخص نموده بکروری تاکید کند که بتحصیل درآورده تحویل فوطه دار نماید و اگر احیاناً محالی از محالات نقایه جات مشخص مانده باشد آن را نیز تشخیص نموده بوصول رساند و آنچه از باقی و تقاوی سنوات در رعایا طلب باشد از مواضع باقیدار بر جمع حال که به تشخیص درآید مبلغ بنحو دو به یک در صد در هر فصل بتحصیل درآید و زر که بصیغه تقاوی در سال گذشته برعایا تنخواه شده باشد تا باقی سالانه بور در اول

توزیع محصول سالحال بگردد در افزونی زراعت و کثرت آبادانی مساعی موفوره بظهور
رساند و محافظت و نگاهبانی زر تحویل فوطه‌دار و جواب مبلغی که از عین المال ثابت برد
زرداو باقی ماند بدستور مقرر بعهده خود دانسته نوعی خبردار باشد که یکدام بدون
سند معتبر دیوان پسند صرف نتواند نمود و تمامی زر تحویل در انجام امور رسانیده
قبض الوصول به فوطه‌دار بدهد و احتیاط بکار برد که به نسبت محصول عمل جاگیرداران
تفاوت بظهور نیاید و یکدام باقی نماند که در صورت التوای معامله و ماندن باقی بازخواست
آن از خواهد شد و هرگاه رعایا به فوطه‌خانه بیارد چهتهای مهر خود و دستخط فوطه‌دار بایشان بدهد تا
هنگام مباقی و اصلات را بموجب همان چهتها محسوب گرداند و سوای زر واجب
بصیغه ابواب ممنوعه نگیرد و از وجه حق التحصیل کروری یکروپیه عوض آن موقوف داشته
داخل جمع نماید که تا فی الحال در برآمد ذمه و مجرا خواهد شد و باقی وجه مذکور را بموجب سند
جداگانه منجمله رعایا و تقاوی که بوصول رسد بدهد و بر تقدیر که زر مذکور تنخواه حق التحصیل [illegible]
قدری را بدر را از تحصیل سالحال تن ناید و در سر رشته کاغذ موافق ضابطه بدفترخانه والا رسانید
باید که چودهریان و قانونگویان و متعدیان و مزارعان و رعایای آنجا خدمت مسطور را [illegible]

دانسته قول و قرار و تشخیص و پرداخت او را منظور و معتبر دانند و از سخن صلاح و صوابدید
او بیرون نروند و شکر و شکایت او را در باره خود با مؤثر دانند خدمت کروری محال
بابیاقی و بازیافت معاش در نیولا خدمت کروری محال با بیاقی و اراضی بازیافت آئمه و معاش
پرگنه فلان سرکار و صوبه فلان از ابتدای فلان بفلان حسب الضمن مقرر شده که لوازم
و مراسم آن خدمت بدیانت و راستی پرداخته با کافه رعایا سلوک پسندیده نماید
و محالی که در بابیاقی آید آن را از قرار واقع بضبط در آورده تا تنخواه شدن بجاگیرداران
مال واجب را موافق آنچه امین بعد ملاحظه جمع سنوات عمل جاگیرداران پیشین وجودات
حال تحریری تمام باستصواب او تشخیص نماید تحصیل نموده تحویل فوطه‌دار نماید و اگر
محالی از محالات لغایه حال مشخص نمانده باشد آن را نیز باصلاح امین تحصیل نماید و آنچه
از باقی و تقاوی سنوات زر در رعایا طلب باشد از مواضع با قید از رجع حال که بسر رشته
تشخیص در آید مبلغ پنج و بیست صد در هر فصل تحصیل در آرد و زری که بصیغه تقاوی در سالگذشته
برعایا تنخواه شده باشد یا باقی سالها بود در اول توزیع محصول سالحال بگیرد و احتیاط
بکار برد که به نسبت محصول عمل جاگیرداران تفاوت بظهور نیاید و یکدام باقی نماند که در صورت

الزام معامله و ماندن باقی از و بازیافت خواهد شد و در که رعایا بفوط خانه بسیار وجهی
آن مهر خود و بخط و خط و دار با تنها به اند و مسکام مهاتی و اصلات الی موجب همان
جهتی محسوب گرداند و سوای واجب جزی بعنیه ابواب ممنوعه بگیرد و از وجه تحصیل الی خود
یکروپیه بر صدی عوض آمد موقوف داشته داخل جمع نماید که تا فی الحال در برآمد
او مجرا خواهد شد و ما بقی وجه مذبور بموجب سند جداگانه منجمد رعایا و تقاوی [illegible] وصول
رسد بتصدیق امین میگرفته باشد و بر تقدیر که زر مذبور به تنخواه حق التحصیل وفا کند قدر زائد
از تحصیل سال الحال بگیرد و سر رشته کاغذ موافق ضابطه بدفترخانه والا برساند باشد
باید که چودهریان و قانونگویان و مزارعان و رعایا آنجا مشار الیه را کروری محال مذبور
دانسته لوازم و لواحق آن خدمت را متعلق شناسند سند خدمت [illegible]
متصدیان مهمات صوبه زین البلاد احمدآباد بدانند در نیولا حسب الحکم اعلی خدمت
رفع ابواب ممنوعه واقعه صوبه مذبور از انتقال فلان بفلان مقرر شده که بلوازم و مراسم
آن براستی و درستی پرداخته دقیقه از دقایق حزم و هوشیاری نامرعی نگذارد و
رفع ابواب ممنوعه آنچه لازمه تقیدست مطابق احکام شریعت غرا بتقدیم رساند

در مسجد بنا کرده قوم اسمعیلیه امام و موذن تعین نماید و منهیات و مسکرات
برطرف سازد و از آن فریق مچلکا بعدم اختلال دعوی مردم بگیرد باید که خدمت
مذبور را الی [illegible] مقرر دانسته لوازم و لواحق آن را متعلق شناسند و در [illegible] تاکید دانند
سند [illegible] داعیهای ملوبخاص در نیولا حسب الحکم مبلغ [illegible] نقد دام پرگنه فلان سرکار
و صوبه فلان که از تغیر فلان [illegible] بابتی خالصه شریفه تعلق یافته من ابتدای فلان [illegible]
ملوبخاص بعهده آن [illegible] مقرر شده باید که از دیاد و آبادانی و تکثیر زراعت و افزونی
محصول سرکار [illegible] رعایا تقید بلیغ بکار برده وجه محصول آنرا [illegible] واقع
بضبط در آورده ملوبخاص موجب [illegible] درست ساخته ارسال حضور پر نور نموده باشد
در نیهاب تاکید داند خدمت راهداری و تهانه داری در نیولا خدمت راهداری و تهانه دار
فلان [illegible] متعلق صوبه فلان از تغیر فلان مطابق ضمن بفلان مقرر شده که بلوازم و مراسم انخدمت
براستی و درستی پرداخته در بندوبست و ضبط و ربط و تنبیه و تادیب مفسدان و [illegible] آن
[illegible] زیردستان و مالگذاران و منع [illegible] اقوی کوشد و احتیاط بکار برد
که [illegible] مرتکب منهیات و مسکرات گردد و محافظت شاهراه نوعی نماید که مسافرین و تردد

بجمعیت خاطر و طمانیت باطن آمد و شد نموده باشند و هیچ جا اثری از دزد و قطاع الطریق ظاهر نشود و اگر مال کسی بدزدی یا بغارت رود آن را بجنس باز دزدان و رهزنان پیدا ساخته مال را بمالک و انجا عه بد مال را بسزا رسانند و در صورت پیدا نساختن از عهده جواب مال مذبور برآید باید که چودهریان و قانونگویان و زمینداران و مقدمان و مزارعان و رعایا را آنجا را مداریها تهانه داری آنجا بعهده مشار الیه مقرر دانسته لوازم و لواحق آن باو متعلق شناسند خدمت امانی تومان پشاور متصدیان مهمات و متکفلان معاملات حال و استقبال و ملکان و مقدمان و مزارعان و رعایا تومان پشاور مضافات صوبه دار الملک کابل بدانند که درینولا حسب الحکم اعلی خدمت امانی تومان پشاور از تغیر فلان بفلان حسب الضمن مقرر شد که بلوازم و مراسم آن از راستی و درستی پرداخته دقیقه از دقایق حزم و هوشیاری غیر مرعی نگذارد و در بند و بست تومان مذبور و استمالت رعایای آنجا مرز و بوم جد و جهد بلیغ بظهور رساند و دیگری را بکار خود شریک نداند و چهل هزار روپیه پیشکش سرکار معلی در هشت سال به قسط پنجهزار روپیه هر سال داخل خزانه صوبه مذبور سازد و رسوم ملکانه و انعام امانی بدستور جمع بندی خود بگیرد و زیاده طمع و توقع نماید باید که خدمت مذبور بمشار الیه مقرر دانسته لوازم و لواحق آن

باو متعلق شناسند و تفریق انعام ملکانه و نانکار و خرج الوتسی و تشخیص و غیره هر نوع الوس و انعام ملکانه و غیره ایشان در باب استصواب موما الیه نموده باشند در ینباب تاکید دانند خدمت داروغگی کچهری دستک باسم متصدیان مهمات و عمله و فعله دیوانی کچهری صوبه فلان آنکه درینولا حسب الحکم اعلی خدمت داروغگی کچهری مذکور از تغیر فلان بفلان مقرر شده که بلوازم و مراسم آن خدمت از راستی و درستی پرداخته دقیقه از دقایق حزم و هوشیاری مهمل و نامرعی نگذارد و تقید نماید که در هیچ معامله از معاملات آنجا فوت و فرو گذاشت میان نیاید و هر رشته کاغذی که از ترکنات برسد از روی آن نسخه دیوانی درست کرده بمعرفت دیوان صوبه سال بسال به فرخانه معلی میرسانیده باشد و هر چه بر ذمه هر کس مطالبه و محاسبه باشد و دیوان صوبه نوشته بدهد بتقید تمام وصول نموده داخل خزانه عامره نماید باید که مشار الیه را داروغه کچهری دانسته لوازم و لواحق آن خدمت باو متعلق شناسند در ینباب تاکید دانند خدمت داروغگی مبیع غلات دستک باسم متصدیان مهمات و عمله و فعله فلان انجا آنکه درینولا خدمت داروغگی مبیع غلات آنجا از تغیر فلان بفلان مقرر شده که بلوازم و مراسم آن براستی و درستی پرداخته

غلات را بروقت موافق نرخ به کفایت تمام مبتی نموده زر قیمت آن از تحویلدار تحویلدار آنها
وتعقید بکار برد که او دامی از تحویل خود بدون سند معتبر دیوان سند خرج نتواند کرد
و تمامی زر تحویل او را بخزانه عامره رسانیده قبض الوصول با وجه باید که مشار الیه را
داروغه مُبتی غلات آنجا دانسته لوازم و لواحق آن را متعلق شناسند و در این باب تاکید دانند
خدمت استیفا دستک باسم فلان آنکه در نیولا خدمت استیفا فلانجا از تغیر
فلان با و مقرر شده که بلوازم و مراسم این خدمت از قرار واقع پرداخته از روی راستی و
درستی در تنقیح محاسبات و مطالبات دقیقه از دقایق خبرسی و هوشیاری
غیر مرعی نگذارد و محاسبه را موافق ضابطه مقرر بدستخط دیوان نصوبه رساند تا موجب
آن بازیافت و بازخواست بعمل آید در این باب تاکید دانسته شناسد خدمت پیشکاری دیوانی فوج
دستک باسم متصدیان مهمات و عمله و فعله دیوانی فوج همراهی فلان آنکه در نیولا
خدمت پیشکاری دیوانی فوج مذبور بفلان مقرر شده که بلوازم و مراسم این خدمت از
قرار واقع پرداخته دقیقه از دقایق حزم و هوشیاری نامرعی نگذارد و ... همراه
و دیگر ارباب طلب در خزانه فوج فراهم آید احتیاط نماید که دامی ... بدون سند معتبر دیوان

به تنخواه در نیاید و در صورت تنخواه شدن بضابطه باز پرس آن ذمه خود
شناسد و نسخه دیوانی و جمع و خرج و استهه خزانه و دیگر سر رشته کاغذ
موافق ضابطه مُنقح و مُفصل درست ساخته بدفترخانه مُعلّی میرسانیده باشد و
با عمله و فعله سلوک پسندیده و شایسته بکار برد باید که آنها خدمت مذکور مشار الیه
مُقرر دانسته لوازم و لواحق آن را متعلق شناسند داروغگی و منهی سایر
دستک باسم متصدیان مهمات و عمله و فعله محال سایر صوبه فلان آنکه در نیولا
حسب الحکم اعلی خدمت داروغگی و امینی محال مذکور از تغیر فلان بفلان مقرر شده که بلوازم
و مراسم این خدمت بدیانت و راستی پرداخته دقیقه از دقایق حزم و احتیاط نامرعی
نگذارد و محصول احتساب و چبوتره چهلبند ... بر طبق قاعده مُعیّن بقید ضبط در آورده تحویلدار
نماید و محافظت و نگهبانی زر تحویل او بعهده خود دانسته نگذارد که دامی بدون سند
معتبر دیوان ... صرف تواند نمود و تمامی زر تحویل او را بخزانه عامره رسانیده قبض الوصول
بازیافت نماید و نگهبانی خیابان ... هنگام شب زیر مهر خود و داروغه نگاه دارد
... خیابان ... محصول متاع خود در آنجا برسد وجه حاصل را موافق ضابطه

مقرر از روباز یافت نماید و احتیاط بکار برد که بیوپاریان هنود اجناس خود را
بنام مسلمین نتوانند نویسانید و محلکار اینمعنی از دلالان آنجا بگیرد باید که آنها
مشارالیه را از روعه با امین آنجا دانسته لوازم و لواحق این خدمت را
متعلق شناسند در سند خدمت کرورانیقدر زیاده باید نوشت که در کرد آوری
رسد مکانات و باکه جات برونجات نوعی تقید بکار برد که قطع رسد بتوقوع نیاید
دستک توپخانه دستک باسم کاشتهای فوجداران و جاگیرداران
و گذربانان و مستحفظان طرق و شوارع آنکه فرد بمهر متصدیان توپخانه برکار والا
بدفتر معلی رسید که بموجب حکم اقدس جانوران با بین اهتمام فلانی وغیره میر شکاران
برای گزیره رکه فلان میروند دستک حضور پرنور در نیباب مرحمت شود دهند
شکارش میرود که هر جا طرفداران مذکور جانوران شکار را فرود آرند لوازم حوالی را
بجا آورده و آنچه از کوتب و گنجشک وغیره برای طعمه مطلوب باشد بلا توقف سرانجام نموده
وجه قیمت آن موافق نرخ روبروبدهانند و احتیاط نمایند که احدی از آنها تعدی
در جایه کسی فرود نیاید و ترکب مضرت و ایذا نشود در خدمت

دستک باسم متصدیان مهمات و عمله و فعله دارالضرب فلانجا آنکه در نیولا خدمت
جوکسائی و وزن کشی طلا و نقره محال مذکور از تغیر فلان بفلان مقرر شده که بلوازم
و مراسم آن مهمات و رستی پرداخته دقیقه از دقایق حزم و هوشیاری نامرعی
نگذارد و در غایت بیوپاریان و نهایت محصول سرکار و الاقرار واقعی بکوشد و اشرفی و
روپیه بوزن مقرر و عیار کامل موافق ضابطه بسکه مبارک میرسانیده باشند سوای
هشتانه اجوره سری هزار روپیه رسوم وزن کشی و جوکسائی موافق معمول قدیم گرفته
زیاده طلبی ننماید باید که مشارالیه را جوکسی و وزنکش محال مذکور دانسته لوازم و لواحق آن
با و متعلق شناسند خدمت قبض نویسی منصبداران دستک باسم متصدیان مهمات و
عمله و فعله خزانه صوبه آنکه در نیولا خدمت قبض نویسی منصبداران آنجا از تغیر فلان بفلان
مقرر شده که بلوازم و مراسم این خدمت از قرار واقع پرداخته دقیقه از دقایق حزم
و هوشیاری نامرعی نگذارد و قبوض منصبداران موافق ضابطه بدفتر معلی میرسانیده باشند
باید که تنها مشارالیه را قبض نویس منصبداران مذکور دانسته لوازم و لواحق آن
با و متعلق شناسند خدمت امینی و دست بدستی روزینه داران و غیره دستک باسم متصدیان

محال سایر شاهگنج درکاب گنج وغیره واقعه دار الخلافه درکاب سعادت انگه

در ینولا خدمت امینی تنخواه دست بدستی روزینه داران و ماهیانه داران

وسالیانه داران آنجا از تغیر فلان بفلان مقرر شده که بلوازم و مراسم آن براستی

و درستی پرداخته دقیقه از دقایق حزم و هوشیاری غیر مرعی نگذارد و از متصدیان

محالات مذبور زر تنخواه جماعه مذبور گرفته بعد تنقیح صحت اسناد و حج العالی اشخاص

و دستکات تنخواه بمهر دیوان صوبه موافق ضابطه دست بدست تنخواه دارا میداده

باشند و قبض الوصول بمهر آنها بستانند و جمع و خرج آن از سال بسال بدفتر معلی رسانند

باید که خان مشار الیه را امین تنخواه دست بدستی دانسته لوازم و لواحق آن

بمشار الیه متعلق شناسند میر بندری فرخنده و داروغگی نمکسار بندر دستک

باسم متصدیان مهمات بندر مبارک سورت مضافات صوبه احمد آباد آنکه در ینولا

حسب الحکم اعلی خدمت میر بندری فرخنده و داروغگی نمکسار بندر مذکور از تغیر

فلان بفلان مقرر شده که بلوازم و مراسم آنخدمت براستی و درستی پرداخته

دقیقه از دقایق حزم و هوشیاری نامرعی نگذارد و سوداگران وغیره را بحسن سلوک خوشنود

بوجهی من الوجوه

و داروغه نمکسار

راضی داشته در گردآوری محصول سرکار والا آنچه لازمه تقید است بتقدیم رساند

و احتیاط بکار برد که در معاملات آنجا فوت و فروگذاشتی بوقوع نیاید باید

که مشار الیه را میر بندر آنجا دانسته لوازم و لواحق آن با و متعلق شناسند

خدمت میر بحری داروغگی نواره دستک باسم متصدیان مهمات و عمله و فعله میر بحری

فلان جا آنکه در ینولا حسب الحکم اعلی خدمت میر بحری آنجا از تغیر فلان بفلان مقرر شده

که بلوازم و مراسم آنخدمت از راستی و درستی پرداخته دقیقه از دقایق

حزم و هوشیاری غیر مرعی نگذارد و دستبهار آن کشتیها شب با حتیاط نگاه دارد

و تقید بکار برد که احدی از مفسدان و متمردان عبور نتواند کرد باید که مشار الیه را

میر بحر آنجا دانسته لوازم و لواحق آن با و متعلق شناسند خدمت امینی گوتوالی

دستک باسم متصدیان مهمات و عمله و فعله چبوتره کوتوالی بلده فلان آنکه

حسب الحکم خدمت امینی چبوتره کوتوالی مذکور از تغیر فلان بفلان مقرر شده که بلوازم

و مراسم آن براستی و درستی پرداخته دقیقه از دقایق حزم و هوشیاری غیر مرعی

نگذارد و به عمله و فعله آنجا سلوک پسندیده نماید و احتیاط بکار برد که در معاملات آنجا

فوت و فروگذاشتی بوقوع نیاید باید که مشار الیه را امین آنجا دانسته لوازم و لواحق
آن را متعلق شناسند خدمت پیشکاری دیوانی صوبه دستک باسم متصدیان
مهمات و عمله و فعله دیوانی صوبه فلان آنکه حسب الحکم اعلی خدمت پیشکاری دیوانی صوبه مذبور
از تغیر فلان بفلان مقرر شده که بلوازم و مراسم آن خدمت بدیانت و راستی پرداخته
دقیقه از دقایق حزم و هوشیاری نامرعی نگذارد و سررشته دفتر دیوانی صوبه مذکور بر وفق
درست داشته نسخه دیوانی و غیره کاغذ مطلوبه را سال بسال مطابق قاعده معین در حضور
معلی رسانیده باشد و نوعی احتیاط و جزرسی بکار برد که در هیچ معامله از معاملات آنجا
فوت و فروگذاشتی بوقوع نیاید باید که مشار الیه را پیشکار دیوانی صوبه مذبور دانسته
لوازم و لواحق آن را متعلق شناسند خدمت داروغگی و ناخدائی جهازات دستک باسم
متصدیان مهمات و متکفلان معاملات و عمله و فعله بندر سورت مبارک صوبه زین البلاد
احمدآباد آنکه در ینولا حسب الحکم اعلی خدمت داروغگی و ناخدائی جهازات بندر معلی
واقعه بندر مذبور مطابق ضمن از تغیر فلان بفلان مقرر شده که بلوازم و مراسم آن خدمات
از راستی و درستی و امانت و دیانت قیام نموده دقیقه از دقایق حزم و هوشیاری

235b

نامرعی نگذارد و با عمله و فعله آنجا طریقه حسن سلوک مسلوک دارد باید که خدمات
مذبوره بعهده مومی الیه مقرر دانسته لوازم و لواحق آن را متعلق شناسند خدمت
دست تصدی او را در اجرای امور مضافه آن قوی دانند خدمت داروغگی خزانه دستک
باسم متصدیان مهمات و عمله و فعله خزانه صوبه فلان آنکه در ینولا حسب الحکم اعلی
خدمت داروغگی خزانه مذکور از تغیر فلان بفلان مقرر گشته که بلوازم و مراسم آن
بدیانت و راستی پرداخته دقیقه از دقایق حزم و هوشیاری و تعهد غیر مرعی نگذارد
و محافظت خزانه قرار واقع نموده باخبر باشد که در دخل و خرج تفاوت و نقصان نباید
و دامی بدون سند معتبر دیوان پسند صرف نشود و زری که فراهم آید در حجره خزانه
نگاه داشته در آن را بمهر خود و خزانچی مقفل داشته بحضور خود بگشاید و ببندد و
نوعی تقید نماید که احدی دست تصرف دراز نتواند کرد باید که مشار الیه را داروغه
خزانه مذبور دانسته لوازم و لواحق آن را متعلق شناسند خدمت جوهری صرافه
دستک باسم متصدیان مهمات و عمله و فعله صرافه بلده فلان آنکه در ینولا خدمت
جوهری صرافه بلده مذکور از تغیر فلان بفلان مقرر شده که بلوازم و مراسم آن خدمت

236a

براستی و درستی پرداخته دقیقه از دقایق حزم و هوشیاری نامرعی نگذارد و
چهره خوش نخرد بل سیاهه متصدیان آنجا میرسانیده باشد و عمله و فعله آنجا را
بحسن سلوک خود راضی داشته زیاده از رسوم مقرری چیزی از صرافان طلب نماید
و بدعتی نو احداث نکند باید که مشار الیه را چوهری صرافه بلده مذبور دانسته
لوازم و لواحق آن را متعلق شناسند و از سخن و صلاح و صوابدید او که هر آینه
متضمن کفایت سرکار والا و رفاهیت رعایا باشد بیرون نروند خدمت مشرفی پرگنه
دستک باسم متصدیان مهمات پرگنه فلان سرکار و صوبه فلان آنکه درینولا خدمت
مشرفی پرگنه مذبور از تغیر فلان بفلان مقرر شده که بلوازم و مراسم انخدمت
براستی و درستی پرداخته دقیقه از دقایق حزم و هوشیاری مهمل و نامرعی نگذارد
و سررشته کاغذ آنجا موافق ضابطه مقرر و قاعده معین نحوی که احکام تفتیش تفاوت
و تجاوز ظاهر نشود درست نموده بدفترخانه معلی میرسانیده باشد و [illegible]
حضور از تحویلدار آنجا بلاتنخواه ندهد و در صورت تنخواه [illegible] شناسند و
عمله و فعله را بحسن سلوک خود راضی داشته در تقدیم ضوابط انخدمت مساعی جمیله

بظهور رساند باید که آنها مشار الیه را مشرف آنجا دانسته لوازم و لواحق
انخدمت را متعلق شناسند خدمت کروری خزانه و نزاولی زر اقساط پرگنه دستک
باسم متصدیان مهمات و عمله و فعله پرگنه فلان سرکار فلان آنکه درینولا خدمت
کروری خزانه و نزاولی زر اقساط پرگنه مذبور از تغیر فلان بفلان مقرر شده که بلوازم
و مراسم انخدمت براستی و درستی پرداخته دقیقه از دقایق حزم و هوشیاری
نامرعی نگذارد و در محافظت خزانه سعی نماید که در دخل و خرج آن تفاوتی بمیان نیاید
و وام و درمی بی سند معتبر دیوان بخرج نرود و نزاولی زر اقساط پرگنه را
بلاتوقف بحضور پرنور میرسانیده باشد باید که مشار الیه را کروری خزانه و نزاولی
زر اقساط پرگنه مذکور دانسته لوازم و لواحق انخدمت را متعلق شناسند خدمت
اخبارنویسی پرگنه دستک باسم فلان آنکه درینولا خدمت اخبارنویسی پرگنه فلان از
تغیر فلان بفلان مقرر شده که بلوازم و مراسم آن از قرار واقع پرداخته دقیقه از
دقایق حزم و هوشیاری نامرعی نگذارد و کیفیت معاملات و مقدمات پرگنه مذبور
بغور و جز رسی تمام مطلع شده سیاهه اخبارات را بلاتفاوت در کم و کاست

تقسیمی که فوت و فرو گذاشت بعمل نیاید درست نموده بحضور پر نور ارسال داشته
باشند درین باب تاکید دانند خدمت داروغگی خزانه و مشرف اولی کاغذ صوبه دستک
باسم متصدیان مهمات صوبه فلان که درینولا حسب الحکم اعلی خدمت داروغگی
خزانه و مشرف اولی ارسال کاغذ صوبه مذبور از تغیر فلان بفلان مقرر شده که لوازم مراسم آن
براستی و درستی پرداخته دقیقه از دقایق حزم و احتیاط و هوشیاری نامرعی نگذارد
و زریکه از تحصیل برکنات و مطالبات و دیگر وجوهات فراهم آید بضابطه معتبر با تعلق
دیوان صوبه و امین در خزانه نگاه دارد و در آنرا بمهر خود مقفل داشته بحضور خود بکشاید
و بربندد و تقید بکار برد که احدی دست تصرف در آن نتواند کرد و خرجی بدون سند
معتبر دیوان سند صرف نشود و سر رشته کاغذ موجودات خزانه مطابق قاعده
هر پانزده روز بحضور پر نور میفرستاده باشد و قدغن نماید که عمال محال خالصه شریفه آن صوبه
در جمع و اصلباقی و دیگر سر رشته کاغذ بضابطه معین و قاعده مقرر درست نموده
بلا توقف و تاخیر معرفت دیوان صوبه مذبور مع علی ارسال دارد [illegible]
داروغه خزانه و مشرف اول کاغذ آنجا دانسته مطابق یرلیغ معلی بعمل آرند

237b

دستک باسم متصدیان مهمات و عمله و فعله چبوتره کوتوالی رکاب سعادت
و بلده دار الخلافه شاهجهان آباد آنکه درینولا خدمت مشرفی بندیخانه چبوتره مذبور از تغیر
فلان بفلان مقرر شده که لوازم و مراسم آن خدمت قرار واقعی پرداخته دقیقه از دقایق
احتیاط و هوشیاری نامرعی نگذارد و سر رشته کاغذ محبوسان بشرح علت قید و سبب
خلاصی آنها موافق ضابطه نگاه دارد باید که او را مشرف بندیخانه دانسته لوازم و لواحق
آن با و متعلق شناسند خدمت مردهائی و دندیه گری نظارت دستک باسم متصدیان
مهمات و عمله و فعله فلان جا آنکه درینولا خدمت مردهائی و دندیه گری نظارت آنجا از تغیر
فلان بفلان مقرر شده که لوازم و مراسم آن براستی و درستی پرداخته دقیقه حزم و احتیاط
نامرعی نگذارد و پیادهای متعینه آنجا را بتعهد تمام درکار پادشاهی حاضر و سرگرم نگهدارد باید
که مشار الیه را میردهها و دندیه یا ناظر آنجا دانسته لوازم و لواحق آن با و متعلق شناسند
حسب الحکم بنام ناظم صوبه [illegible] بعد تحریر القاب درینولا فلانی و غیره اهوان مبلغ [illegible] نقد
[illegible] دستگردان از خزانه عامره رکاب سعادت نموده اند و عوض آن
مبلغ مذبور [illegible] روپیه وجه [illegible] انعام [illegible] المقطع از خراج [illegible] البلاد [illegible]

238a

تنخواه حکم شده لهذا حسب الحکم اقدس اعلی قلمی میگردد که آن امارت و ایالت مرتبت
مبلغ مذکور را بموجب پروانه حضور پرنور که بنام دیوان صوبه شرف صدور یافته زود
تنخواه بدهانند درینباب از جناب عالمیان مآب تاکید اکید دانند حسب الحکم بنام دیوان صوبه
بنگاله بعد تحریر القاب درینولا فلانی وغیره ساهوان مبلغ اینقدر لک روپیه بطریق دستگردان
داخل خزانه عامره رکاب سعادت نموده اند عوض آن مبلغ مذکور مبلغ اینقدر هزار روپیه وجه هندوان
وانعام شده با مبلغ المقطع از خزانه صوبه جنت البلاد بنگاله تنخواه حکم شده لهذا قلمی میگردد
که آن شهامت مرتبت مبلغ مذکور را حسب الضمن بعد وضع دو سرخه بلا توقف تنخواه داده
وقبض بمهر ساهوان ستانند تا فی الحال بموجب همین پروانه قبض الوصول مجرا محسوب
خواهد گردید درینباب تاکید دانند پروانه کاشت زمین بنجر بضابطه در قصبات مهمات
حال و استقبال پرگنه فلان سرکار و صوبه فلان بدانند درینولا فلانی التماس نمود که در پرگنه
مذکور زمین افتاده خارج جمع بسیار است اگر از جمله آن اینقدر بیگهه بضابطه کم دستور بطریق
استمرار حواله بنده شود آنرا مزروع ساخته محصول واجب را بسرکار ... مقرر گرداند
میرسانیده باشد از آنجا که رفاه خلق الله و آبادی ملک منظور نظر ...

لهذا قلمی میگردد که از جمله زمین بنجر افتاده خارج جمع موازی اینقدر بیگهه در صورتیکه مالش کسی
حاضر نباشد یا باوجود حضور از عهده سرانجام آن نمیتواند برآمد بمشار الیه حواله نمایند که بقدر
استطاعت خود دشتکار نماید و محصول آنرا در سال اول پنجم حصه و در سال دوم چهارم حصه
و از سال سوم سیوم حصه بطریق استمرار ازو میگرفته باشند و بعلت اخراجات دیگر
بوجهی من الوجوه مزاحمت نرسانند و احتیاط نمایند که عوض زمین بنجر افتاده خارج جمع زمین مزروعه
نتواند گرفت و اگر فی الحال خلاف آن ظاهر شود از ابتدای تصرف لغایته تاریخی که خلاف
بظهور رسید کم دستور را موافق دستور محصول زمین زرعی نصف بازیافت نمایند
تا باعث عبرت دیگران گردد درینباب تاکید اکید دانند ضابطه معافی محصول اگر دخل و
خرج مساوی یا دخل از خرج کم باشد بعلت محصول مزاحمت نرسانند و اگر دخل از خرج زیاده
باشد ششم حصه از مسلمین و چهارم حصه از هنود بستانند لهذا قلمی میگردد که درینباب
موافق ضابطه صدر بعمل آرند خدمت نزاولی ارسال زر و سرشته کاغذ پرگنه دستک بنام
شجاعت حشمت فلانی آنکه چون خدمت نزاولی تاکیدات زر سرکار معلی و ارسال کاغذ
پرگنه فلان از صوبه فلان بعهده او مقرر شده باید که بلوازم و مراسم آن خدمت قرار واقع

ساهوان

پرداخته دقیقه از دقایق حزم و هوشیاری غیر مرعی نگذارد و ذریعهٔ تحصیل آن محال و آمد
با مین آنجا تاکید نماید که بر سبیل هندویات معتبر بحضور انور ارسال دارد و کاغذ و جمع
جمع واصل باقی و غیره بحضور لامع النور میفرستاده باشد نگذارد که در ارسال کاغذ و ترسیل زر توقف
و تعلل بمیان آید در خیانت تاکید داند ۱۱ دستک تنخواه درماهه دخرج مقرری آن خزانهٔ عامره
دستک باسم مشرف و تحویلدار خزانچی خزانهٔ عامرهٔ رکاب سعادت آنکه حسب الحکم اعلی
مبلغ پانصد روپیه درماهه رفعت پناه فلان بصیغهٔ دخرج از ابتدای فلان از تحویل او
تنخواه شده باید که او وجه درماهه خانمشار الیه را از ابتدای صدر بعد گرفتن قبض الوصول
بدستور دیگر تنخواهداران مقرری آنجا موافق ضابطه ماه بماه تنخواه میداده باشد که
تا فی الحال مطابق این دستک و قبض الوصول بحساب او مجرا و محسوب خواهد شد شرح دستک
تنخواه کارخانه دواب دستک باسم فلان خزانچی آنکه مبلغ ده هزار روپیه در وجه
خوراک و غیره اسپان اصطبل یا فیلان فیلخانه یا دیگر کارخانه دواب تحویل فلان تحویلدار
من ابتدای فلان از تحویل او تنخواه شده باید که مبلغ مذبور از تحویل خود به تحویل تحویلدار فلانی
نموده قبض الوصول بمهر متصدیان کارخانه مسطور بستاند که تا فی مطابق این دستک و قبض الوصول

از حساب

در حساب او مجرا و محسوب خواهد شد دستک تنخواه درماهه منصبدار از محال سایر دستک
باسم متصدیان کوتهه پارچه یا شاه گنج یا دیگر محال سایر آنکه مبلغ اینقدر روپیه درماهه
فلان منصبدار فرقه فلان متعینه مکان فلان از ابتدای فلان از محصول آنجا تنخواه شده
باید که آنها وجه مشار الیه را از ابتدای صدر بدستور دیگر تنخواهداران مقرری آنجا
موافق ضابطه تنخواه میداده باشند و قبض الوصول تحویلدار آنجا بدهند که تا فی الحال
مطابق این دستک و قبض الوصول در حساب آنها مجرا و محسوب خواهد شد ۱۱